51

ASHES '85

ASHES '85

MATTHEW ENGEL

with photographs by
Graham Morris

PELHAM BOOKS

First published in Great Britain by
Pelham Books Ltd
44 Bedford Square
London WC1B 3DP
1985

ISBN 0 7207 1645 4

Typeset, printed and bound in Great Britain by
Butler & Tanner Ltd, Frome, Somerset

CONTENTS

INTRODUCTION

This is an account of the Ashes series of 1985, and ancillary matches, more or less as it was reported in the pages of the *Guardian* at the time. The effect on the reader should be the reverse of the customary work of fiction: most readers will be well aware what happens in the end; the writer, at the time, had not got a clue.

It was awfully tempting to try and do something about this when I was putting the book together, to amend the rushed judgments imposed by a newspaper deadline with the luxuries of hindsight. I have resisted with a fair amount of nobility.

Not everything is quite as it appeared in the paper. The account of the fourth day of the Lord's test never appeared at all, because the *Guardian* did not come out. Sod's Law ensured that this was just about the best day of the series. And I have changed a few things: when I got facts or figures wrong, for instance, which happens; when the *Guardian* made a printing error, which happens less often than some people make out; and when the *Guardian* sub-editor's view of what should appear differed from mine, which happens far less often than it would on any other paper in the business. I have also tidied up a few of my own infelicities – when I realised that what I thought at the time could have been better expressed. But, honest, no hindsight.

I am grateful to everyone on the best sports desk in journalism for their support and indulgence, especially John Samuel and Frank Keating, who has been a constant source of encouragement over the past six years; and also to Dick Douglas-Boyd, Abigail Larter, John Dorman, Graham Morris, Graeme Wright, David Frith and Jacki Warbrook. My thanks too to all my colleagues in the press box, English and Australian, who have provided comradeship, help and kindness – not to mention jokes they knew would never get in their own papers.

Matthew Engel, September 1985

Early warming: Greg Matthews, heavily sweatered in the outfield at Worcester, begins the struggle against the English summer. His breakdancing was a personal extra.

THE EARLY WEEKS

Thursday 2 May

The 1985 Australian cricketers arrived in London yesterday and immediately had their baggage van towed away by the police. It is good to note that, the South Africa business notwithstanding, we have got over any nonsense about feeling sorry for them. This is war, same as usual.

When the team made it to their hotel, Bob Merriman, the manager, squelched the first, obvious and unsubtle questions by saying that any inquiries about South Africa would have to be directed to the Australian Cricket Board in Melbourne. Recent evidence suggests that might not be the best place to discover what is going on, but Merriman was right to try and get everyone off his own and the team's back. The last thing Australia need is for this tour to be polluted the way the 1977 tour was by the Packer defections.

The captain Allan Border was just as firm when someone asked if this was a Second XI: 'No way in the world,' he replied. And it is indeed hard to see how the loss of three players, two of them probable reserves, is as grievous as some people are trying to make out. The danger to Australia is the turmoil that might be going on beneath the surface.

The defections have helped add to the team's recognisability. Jeff Thomson was there, hair bleached, expression fixed, along with the other replacements, Dave Gilbert and Ray Phillips, who have not had time to get green blazers yet. Thomson may well be the only player even regular followers of the game will pick out at this stage, but some of the others will become very easy to spot. There is Greg Matthews, whose punk haircut, as one sage pointed out, makes him look as though he is about to be transported to Australia rather than having just flown over.

David Boon, Tasmania's gift to the tour: 'Marsh without the soft edges.'

The one with the Zapata moustache is David Boon; the silvery-haired gent is the leg-spinner Bob Holland; and the fast bowler Craig McDermott looks like a Great White Hope for the heavyweight crown, which in a sense is what he is. Merriman looks a bit like Bob Hawke, though Hawke probably has the less demanding job.

Border, who is starting to bear an increasing resemblance to Ian Chappell, was particularly defiant in his defence of Thomson. 'If you gentlemen keep criticising him, he is going to have one hell of a summer. He can bowl a very brisk medium pace now and move the ball around, which is going to be very useful.'

Thomson is the only survivor from either the 1975 or 1977 tours, except for Geoff Dymock, who was here in '77 and is now the assistant manager. Dymock, Border, the vice-captain Andrew Hilditch and Geoff Lawson will be the tour selectors, while Merriman concentrates on administration. Their first job will be to pick a team to play Lavinia, Duchess of Norfolk's XI at Arundel on Sunday. The Duchess has had an even harder job raising a team than the Australians did. All but one of the first-class counties have matches that day and the exception, Derbyshire, are playing the previous day at Aberdeen. So the Duchess's team will be captained by Bob Willis and will also include the new professional at Whalley in the Ribblesdale League, one Laxman Sivaramakrishnan.

Before then the Australians have three days of nets at Lord's. Yesterday the players were free to recover from the flight and have their first look round (Ray Phillips and Simon O'Donnell had never been to England before and were most excited). The press meanwhile hung on for the first shareout of the sponsors' lager. I fear the Australians even when they bring gifts.

SOMERSET v. THE AUSTRALIANS
FIRST DAY

Taunton, Thursday 9 May

The first formal business of the 1985 Australian tour after the light workout at Arundel, produced a day's cricket straight out of the Golden Age, although it is hard to imagine many days even then being quite as golden as this one.

It was lovely and breezy and spring in the West, and for two sessions at Taunton the Australian batsmen, led by their captain Allan Border, produced some quite captivating stroke play in the sunshine. Then Border, astonishingly, declared and set up a duel between his own bowlers and Botham from which Botham emerged the winner – provisionally at any rate.

The bare facts are that Somerset finished the day on 151 for four in response to the Australians' 356 for seven. That means 507 runs in the 6½-hour day; 334 of those came in boundaries, 73 fours and seven sixes. It will be remembered that 334 was one of Bradman's scores, and there was much that Bradman would have appreciated about the whole day. If this is the shape of the season ahead, it is going to be quite a summer.

But it had looked as if the Australians would themselves score 500 – or more. At lunch they already had 197 and one was starting to wonder about the 721 in a day scored by the 1948 Australians at Southend. Everything was set up for the batsmen: the outfield was fast, the pitch was friendly, and so was the bowling. Various absences meant that three-fifths of the Somerset attack was inexperienced. Of the exceptions, one was Botham, who bowled two short, sharp spells but otherwise stood at slip and let Marks take the heat.

England's 82–83 tour began with Marks being hit all over the place by a Queensland player, Harry Frei. This tour started with another one, Border, striking him for four straight sixes into and over the old pavilion.

Border's Bradman touch was thus mixed in with a hint of Arthur Wellard. He scored 106 in 102 minutes, reaching his century off 103 balls; he might have passed Botham's 76-ball fastest 100 of the season had not Botham himself come back after lunch and slowed him up a fraction. But all the Australian batsmen looked in remarkable touch one week into their tour.

Wessels played some fine shots, in his crabby style. So did Hilditch, more briefly. Wellham drove handsomely in between Border's assaults. Boon looks like Marsh without the soft edges, and hit the ball very hard. Phillips showed some delightful touches. England must hope they are all peaking too soon.

When anything did happen for Somerset, Botham was involved: he had Hilditch caught in the hook, long-leg, thank-you trap, and Wellham at wide mid-on. The other two wickets went to his catches: Wessels one-handed at slip, then Border when he insisted on getting under a skyer that a normal player, or a less engaged Botham, would have left to Rose. But most of the time 5,000 spectators and 11 Somerset players could only watch as the total piled higher. The sky seemed the limit.

Then Border did the kindly thing. He has said he intends to win every county match, if necessary at the expense of players' practice, and the way to do that seemed to be to put the score beyond reasonable doubt. Still it was a positive decision, and even 207 to avoid the follow-on looked mountainous for a while.

Forty minutes before the close Somerset were 65 for four. Lawson had gradually worked his way to full pelt and Thomson had sent down a flurry of bouncers, several of them decidedly sharp. Then, simultaneously, two very young men took centre stage: the

20-year-old Australian fast bowler McDermott against Richard
Harden, a batsman from Bridgwater, aged 19 and making his
debut because Julian Wyatt has german measles.

Alas, poor Harden, and all his dreams of starting like Gimblett.
He faced seven balls, four of them very, very fast and the last
finishing, off the edge, in Phillips's gloves. At that moment, with
40 minutes left, a familiar figure in a white helmet stamped down
the dressing-room steps. The memories now were not of Edward
VII or Bradman or scrumpy at a penny a pint, but of 1981.

McDermott was bowling so fast that the slips had retreated to
become short third men. Botham took him on. He hooked and
drove and when he got up the other end began to give the Border
treatment to the leg-spinner Holland. McDermott became rattled
and Brian Rose became inspired; he hit six off-side fours from the
lad's last two overs. On came the off-spinner Matthews. Botham
hit three more fours, two cuts and a whopping drive.

His 50 came off 30 balls: 10 fours, one six. It was Headingley
'81 again in excitement, in intensity, in the change-round and in
Botham's dominance. Border said later that the Australians will
rethink their bowling tactics. Come early today if you are anywhere near: it is wonderful stuff.

SECOND DAY

Taunton, Friday 10 May

The magical once-upon-a-time-in-the-West quality went out of the
Australian match at Taunton yesterday and the cricket reverted a
little nearer to business as usual. There were still 445 runs in the
day, which is amazing going by any standards except those of
Wednesday. However, 156 of these came from Kepler Wessels,
who is an exceptionally good batsman but not exactly Cheerful
Charlie. And the day was overladen with sadness when Brian
Rose, close to a century himself, had his arm broken by a short
ball from McDermott.

At the end of the second day the Australians were 282 for six
in their second innings, 324 ahead. Somerset can expect a declaration early this morning. However, all the calculations will depend
on who turns up at the ground today.

Somerset were themselves short of eight of last year's first-team squad even before Rose was hit. The Australians, meanwhile, have been struck by two separate outbreaks of 'flu. Wayne Phillips has one strain and may be out for a week, Lawson has another. Several others, including the captain, Border, have been showing what might be early symptoms. The management will watch the players coming down to breakfast this morning more anxiously than usual.

Several of those Australians still standing will, however, be well pleased with themselves. Top of the list must come Wessels, who was livid when he missed out the previous day and made up for it with what is most unlikely to be his last big century of the summer. In these ideal batting conditions, even a stayer like Wessels could score quickly: 160 minutes to 100, a run a minute thereafter. He dominated the opening stand of 125 with Hilditch then broke away from his customary offside scoring area and joined the 'I've hit a six off Vic' club as did Thomson and, most surprisingly, Holland, whose 35 was only five short of his best ever.

Holland had a busy day, bowling his leg breaks all morning and taking four wickets, including that of Botham, whose epic innings went on for only 10 more balls and 12 more runs before he was stumped for 65 having the most fearful legside wipe. Botham might well have regretted his generosity in allowing the Australians to bend the rules and use their reserve specialist wicket-keeper, Ray Phillips, to deputise for his namesake.

Somerset still got plenty more runs. Marks will never be confused with his own namesakes, Trumper and Ludorum, but he played his short-arm shots to great effect and even hooked a four off Thomson. Rose, meanwhile, was going very well on 81. Then it happened.

Rose is only 34 but with his England place and the Somerset captaincy long gone, his enthusiasm has ebbed, especially when it comes to getting in line against the quickest bowlers, which is understandable but made it ironic as well as sad when McDermott

---

Wayne Phillips in action, with that look of surprise that often characterised his wicket-keeping. Phillips's batting was one of the delights of the season but, well, Australia has sent better 'keepers.

The reserve wicket-keeper's lot is not always a happy one: few chances, little recognition and here no leg stump. Ray Phillips is bowled by Gooch at Chelmsford.

found his right forearm outside leg stump. Rose says it was a good ball and that he bore no grudge. He will be in plaster for five weeks and out of the game for at least eight. There have been rumours that this might be Rose's last season and it is just possible that we have seen the last of the skilful and unlucky cricketer. One hopes not.

Holland, meanwhile, removed most of the later batsmen in more conventional fashion. The breeze was still strong and colder than on Wednesday but it had veered round enough to help Holland's drift and, although hardly anything turned, no one collared him.

Wicket-taking was harder for Somerset. Botham again bowled tastily, but only briefly. Marks and Booth had to buy their wickets and Wessels came very expensive, although he eventually skyed a catch to mid-on. Even he was struggling, with a knee injury. But if he can drag himself and 10 other healthy Australians to the first Test next month, England are going to have to find ways of getting rid of him.

THIRD DAY

Taunton, Saturday 11 May

This may be the right moment to temper the widespread perception that England can regain the Ashes this summer without much trouble. The Australians showed on Wednesday and Thursday how well they can bat. Yesterday they proved how well they can bowl when they dismissed Somerset for 125 to win their opening first-class match in England by 233 runs. Thomson, the umpteenth-choice fast bowler for this tour, took six for 44.

The only thing the Australians cannot do at present is catch. Six chances went down yesterday – Roebuck, who went on to carry his bat, was put down on 10, 11 and 12. They still won with three hours to spare. You have to be impressed.

It looks as though Australia are going to have the two, maybe even the three, fastest bowlers in the Test series ahead. Thomson, despite all Border's pre-tour baloney about what a good medium pacer he is these days, looked very much quicker than that to the Somerset batsmen. The sight of padded Poms has evidently taken years off him. Thomson himself said he had never bowled better in England.

But his figures were made largely at the expense of 20-year-old McDermott, 14 years his junior and clearly something special. He extracted pace and bounce from a pitch that had produced 952 runs on the first two days. Four of the misses came off his bowling, three of them by Wellham at third slip. The ball after Wellham had put Roebuck down for the second time would have been a catch to gully had he been in closer. At this point, McDermott looked down the pitch at Roebuck and said something along the lines of Lawson's 'Christ, do you play for the first team regular?' I dread to think what he said to Wellham.

Roebuck stayed on to play an innings of decidedly first-team character and determination on a day when only two other Somerset batsmen emerged with credit or double figures. You have to remember that Rose had a broken arm and could not bat; but you also have to remember that Lawson, the No. 1 fast bowler, was ill and that Gilbert, no slouch either, has yet to appear. The England batsmen might yet find that the memories of Garner and Marshall are not as far behind them as they thought. Holland turned some of his leg-breaks too, and England did not have to worry about that last summer.

Somerset's theoretical job yesterday was to score 359 in $5\frac{1}{2}$ hours, or a minimum of 80 overs. After four overs they were 15 for two, plus Rose. Both Popplewell and Ollis appeared to be beaten for pace as much as anything else. Thanks to the fielders, there was a bit of a stand when Richard Harden, the debutant from Bridgwater, made up for his first innings nought by resisting for 15 overs against the still-new ball.

But none of the Somerset players, except Roebuck, suggested permanence. McDermott went off and Thomson was granted the downwind end. And, although the official Australian players found it too cold for catching, the substitutes made up for them. Ray Phillips, deputising for the other Phillips as wicketkeeper, took the first of his four catches to remove Harden. Botham came in. Four balls and one off-drive to the boundary later he tried to drive off the back foot at Thomson and only gloved it towards Phillips. Botham departed.

There was still Marks, and he played a vigorous, almost jaunty

SOMERSET v. AUSTRALIANS SCOREBOARD

AUSTRALIANS

K. C. Wessels c Botham b Marks	41	c Botham b Booth	156
A. M. Hilditch c Davis b Botham	20	c Harden b Booth	46
D. M. Wellham c Davis b Botham	64	(7) not out	26
A. R. Border c Botham b Marks	106		
D. C. Boon not out	56	(8) not out	21
W. B. Phillips not out	62		
G. R. J. Matthews		(3) c Roebuck b Booth	22
C. J. McDermott		(4) c sub (Bail) b Marks	0
J. R. Thomson		(5) lbw Marks	7
R. G. Holland		(6) c Popplewell b Booth	35
G. F. Lawson			
Extras (lb 7)	7	(lb 2, nb 1)	3
Total for four declared	356	for six declared	316

Fall of wickets: 47, 85, 221, 248

Fall of wickets: 125, 173, 179, 191, 264, 273

Bowling: Davis 14–2–71–0; Turner 15–0–85–0; Botham 12–3–28–2; Marks 25–4–87–2; Popplewell 3–0–21–0; Booth 11–1–57–0.

Bowling: Botham 6–2–16–0; Davis 7–0–32–0; Turner 11–1–58–0; Marks 28–6–110–2; Booth 22–2–98–4

SOMERSET

P. M. Roebuck c W. Phillips b Lawson	13	not out	33
N. F. M. Popplewell c Boon b Thomson	25	lbw b McDermott	0
R. L. Ollis run out	11	lbw b Thomson	4
B. C. Rose rtd hurt	81	(11) absent hurt	0
R. J. Harden c W. Phillips b McDermott	0	(4) c sub (R. Phillips) b Thomson	17
I. T. Botham st sub (R. Phillips) b Holland	65	(5) c sub (R. Phillips) b Thomson	4
V. J. Marks c sub (R. Phillips) b Holland	50	(6) c sub (R. Phillips) b Thomson	48
T. Gard c Wessels b Holland	30	(7) c sub (Gilbert) b Holland	0
M. S. Turner b Thomson	9	(8) c sub (R. Phillips) b Thomson	0
M. R. Davis st sub (R. Phillips) b Holland	11	(9) c Holland b Thomson	4
S. C. Booth not out	4	(10) c Boon b Holland	5
Extras (b 4, lb 4, nb 7)	15	(b 4, lb 1, nb 5)	10
Total all out	314	all out	125

Fall of wickets: 34, 54, 65, 65, 170, 249, 273, 294, 308, 314

Fall of wickets: 10, 15, 43, 49, 111, 113, 114, 118, 125

Bowling: Thomson 17–5–75–2; Lawson 8–2–31–1; Holland 29.3–11–87–4; McDermott 11–1–71–1; Matthews 9–0–42–0

Bowling: McDermott 12–2–46–1; Thomson 14–1–44–6; Holland 17.1–5–30–2

Umpires: R. Julian and D. R. Shepherd

Australians won by 233 runs

innings of 48 in 54 minutes. Eventually Phillips did for him as well. The rest followed very quickly, Holland and Boon finishing the innings off with two quite decent catches. Roebuck became the first Somerset batsman since Frank Lee in 1934 to carry his bat against a touring team.

After making allowances for weather that would mean mid-winter in Sydney or Brisbane, Border denounced his fielders, not for the first time. Someone has worked out that at home this last season the Australians put down 53 catches in Tests and internationals. 'Not good enough,' Border said. The team will be working on it at Worcester this weekend. But most things, except the fielders' hands, are coming together very nicely for the Australians.

THE CAPTAINCY QUESTION

Monday 20 May

This is Captaincy Week in the *Guardian*. On Wednesday we start to serialise the Thoughts of Brearley, which is likely to become the all-time classic on the subject; so it seems opportune to preface that with a few more ephemeral thoughts, on the England captaincy as it stands in the wake of Gower's somewhat tenuous re-appointment, for the one-day Internationals and the first two Tests only.

It would be nice to start with a plug and tell you that the Brearley book unzips a magic formula, both for winning the Ashes and restoring the fortunes of Piddletrenthide Thirds: 'Praise God and pass the heavy roller', or something. It does not. The book is about common sense uncommonly applied, which was and is the Brearley way.

The problem as far as England are concerned (apart from working out which of our leading modern professionals might trouble to read the book) is discovering who might not only have the sense and be able to apply it, but can play the game well enough to be in a position to do so.

There is a captain capable of all this. Gower is a true son of the game, and it is only three months since his great triumph in India.

But already the doubts are back. At 28, he could in theory be England captain into the 21st century. Yet there is a widespread and, I think, growing feeling that we have yet another short-term incumbent.

So much of the zest has gone from Gower since he became captain. I may be partially responsible myself, along with the rest of the media. No one else in sport is subject to the same sustained national scrutiny. A failing England soccer manager has to stare back at the cameras on half-a-dozen nights a year; and he would be 20 or more years older than Gower without the problems of playing himself.

Gower has an exceptionally hard job; he accepted the challenge, rather than relished it. Perhaps in his own mind he already has a date when he would like to pack it in, although it is more likely to be the 1987 World Cup rather than the Lord's Test next month, which marks the end of his current contract. An outside observer might regard that as sensible, giving him the chance to concentrate once again on what he does best in life, i.e. bat. His agent, knowing that the captaincy can be worth £40,000 a year in advertising deals, might not.

I do not believe the Gower captaincy is close to its end. He has many of the right attributes: he can play, he is bright, he is amiable, his players respect him, and he respects them and is receptive to their ideas. But he is not a profound thinker about cricket; he needs good advisers. And here we hit upon one of the most interesting aspects of this potentially fascinating season.

There have been two major phases to the Gower regime so far: disastrous West Indian summer and successful Indian winter. One major difference was the nature of the opposition. But another was the nature of his chief of staff. Last summer there was Botham but, except in one Test, no Gatting. In winter there was Gatting but no Botham. This summer there will be both, and the makings of a cricketing eternal triangle.

Gower has a long-standing respect for and friendship with both men. But Gatting and Botham are not close friends, and there has been rivalry between them as players ever since the 77–78 tour to Pakistan where they were the two young hopeful all-rounders. Botham made the grade as a Test cricketer at once; Gatting took seven years. And it may well be that Botham's absence was a

major help when he finally established himself at Bombay and Madras; the great man is not always the easiest colleague.

As the years have passed, they have developed very different outlooks on the game. Botham is a believer; Gatting is more of a thinker – he counts the cards and weighs the percentages. Gatting would never have won the Headingley and Edgbaston Tests in '81, as a player or probably as a leader. But I know whose direction would be likely to win more Tests in the future.

One or two posh paper writers this summer have written grave articles about Botham, considering Cowdrey and Ellison and so on, and solemnly concluding that Botham is better than them and should be restored to the team. The subject has always seemed to me unworthy of discussion. Of course, Botham must come back; he is a great cricketer, and now a refreshed one. But England need Botham and Gower and Gatting, all contributing productively and sparking off each other.

And I am increasingly inclined to think that, in the longish term, Gatting may well be the man who can best apply the lessons of Brearley and lead the revival of English cricket. What we need to know first, though, is whether Gatting and Botham can work together.

There are possible captains beyond Gower and Gatting but they remain just that, possible. Cook of Northamptonshire and Cowdrey of Kent have been found wanting as Test cricketers. The Kent committee has presumably done for Cowdrey's predecessor, Tavare. Barnett of Derbyshire and Neale of Worcestershire (who announced his retirement from football to concentrate on cricket over the weekend) were both discussed seriously for last winter's tour, but both need to establish themselves further. Likewise, this week's MCC captain, Nicholas of Hampshire.

Two of the most interesting characters among the county captains are Ontong of Glamorgan and Abrahams of Lancashire, both South African-born but England-qualified. Connoisseurs of

---

Botham and Viv Richards flank Tim Hudson outside Hudson's shop in Prestbury, Cheshire. Hudson was one of the more implausible characters of the summer of '85, becoming Botham's agent (or, as the tabloids kept saying, his millionaire agent) with grand plans to take Botham to Hollywood and turn him into the new Errol Flynn, or something.

man-of-the-match ceremonies will recall how smitten Peter May was by Abrahams at last year's B and H final. But the same objection applies to them as to the other three, plus the thought that a Greig-scarred establishment is unlikely to put a South African in charge of anything again, even if Sir Michael Edwardes somehow happened to score 3,000 first-class runs this season.

All this discussion remains theoretical, for a few weeks at least; all being well with Gower, for a good while longer. It was after the Lord's Test four years ago that Alec Bedser called Brearley from a phone box and asked him back for his finest hour. By the time this year's Lord's Test is over, England should be leading Australia 2–0 with the help of a couple of brilliant centuries by Gower. Bothamesque faith has its place, you know.

MCC v. THE AUSTRALIANS
FIRST DAY

Lord's, Thursday 23 May

The county champions' visit to Lord's in April is traditionally a three-sweater match. MCC v. the Australians is definitely a three-initial match, with MCJ Nicholas in charge of Marylebone's affairs and the private boxes leased out to a variety of improbable up-market names.

However, the Australians' attempt to go one initial too far was quashed very quickly yesterday when MCC insisted that the XXXX beer banner had to come down from their balcony. The players reacted in the time-honoured manner of colonials when faced with stuffy Poms. MCJ asked them to bat; they scored 377 for six, with centuries for both the captain Allan Border and the 22-year-old all-rounder Simon O'Donnell. Do not underestimate this team.

The bowlers, who might very well have been picked as England B, were treated with contempt, especially by Border, who has now scored three centuries in his only three first-class innings. Whatever the surgeons did to his knee last week, he has carried on exactly where he left off at Taunton and Worcester. Viv Richards usually reacts with double centuries if you start to call anyone else the best batsman in the world, but there is certainly no one anywhere batting better than Border.

His problem is that he cannot find a nucleus of men around him batting a fraction as well. The only decent support yesterday came from O'Donnell, of whom more anon, and the ubiquitous Wessels, both of whom had already shown signs of form. I have a recurring nightmare that every time I look up this summer Wessels will be there, steering the ball backward of point for one or two.

But before O'Donnell came in, the Australians were 166 for five and had problems. Hilditch was bowled by a Sidebottom nip-backer in the fourth over and now has only 105 runs in seven innings. If this goes on it will be most distressing to the captain, who may be forced to bat No. 3 (which, like Gower, he prefers to avoid) though even more distressing to Hilditch, who is the vice-captain and a selector himself.

Wood, his opening partner, scratched around all morning, and was just starting to show some confidence after lunch when he hardly played at Willey and was leg before. Wessels was eventually caught at second slip; Ritchie, as seems to be his wont, played a few very good shots then a bad one; Wellham was very neatly caught down the legside by French.

At this stage MCC could feel pleased with themselves, and Sidebottom was bowling well enough to suggest that he might be moving through the ruck towards a place in the one-day Inter-nationals. He is a very English sort of bowler who moves the ball around at briskish pace and, at 31, seems to be getting better and better. Since he has no names at all except Sidebottom and Arnold, he may not go down well in the Lord's boxes, and his appealing has a very Australian mean streak. But he far outshone Neil Williams, who had problems with over-stepping, and Dave Thomas, who had one of his most innocuous days.

But by mid-afternoon, when O'Donnell joined Border, any dampness had gone from the pitch. The Australians brought O'Donnell in the belief that anything Botham can do, he can do, well, almost as effectively, and they may be right. Until this team arrived, O'Donnell had never set foot in England, but he looks as made for conditions here as Barnsley's Arnie. In style, he is more like young Robert Bailey, front-footed and free-swinging, than Botham, but he bowls too, and Lord's never bothered him one bit.

Border took 188 minutes for his century, the slowest of his three. O'Donnell beat him by 20 minutes. Between them they hit 21 off the over when Sidebottom took the new ball, which gave one pause for thought, and four sixes off poor old Underwood. Border was dropped once, on 53 at second slip by Gooch, who was wearing what appeared to be a sweater from his old South African team, Western Province.

He may have been making a point, although I prefer to think it was only that he was cold. Otherwise, Border batted the way Gooch would like to do today, using his arms, his feet and his head and, as with his two previous hundreds, he was trying to get himself out when he finally succeeded. When O'Donnell reached his 100 half an hour before the close, Border declared.

This was not quite so smart. The light had started to go. Gooch and Fowler emerged together for the first of perhaps many big occasions, reached the middle, peered at Lawson through the murk, and at a word from the umpires, turned smartly on their heels and went back inside to scattered boos and ironic applause from Border.

SECOND DAY

Lord's, Friday 24 May

It was another batsmen's day at Lord's yesterday, despite murky light that hung around throughout and curtailed play by almost an hour. Mark Nicholas, the MCC captain, and Allan Lamb scored centuries to cancel out those made by Border and O'Donnell on Wednesday. Nicholas then declared to set up the possibility of a good finish today; the Australians are 125 ahead with one wicket down. His innings may have wider significance.

It is still absurdly premature to talk of Nicholas, on the strength of a career average of just over 30 and a handful of games as Hampshire captain, as an immediate contender to lead England. But as Gower shifts uneasily in the throne room in a manner that would have seemed unbelievable when he left India in February, Nicholas's progress must constitute a disturbing footfall on the stairs outside.

Like Lamb, he has a wonderful sense of timing, which is not

just a matter of striking the ball at the right moment but of knowing that 100 here can be worth 250 at Swansea or somewhere.

Lamb's 122 not out was his third successive hundred at Lord's, after two in Tests last summer; Nicholas's 115 not out is his third successive big score for MCC, after 76 not out and 121 in the last two MCC v. Champions matches. Perhaps they will offer him a permanency: MCJ of MCC – it has a ring to it.

Lamb and Nicholas put on 239 in 50 overs for the third wicket

Gooch and Fowler go out to open MCC's batting against the Australians at Lord's. It was a big day for them both: Gooch back in the big time after three wilderness years; Fowler getting the chance to open with Gooch and prove to himself that he was a real international opener and not just someone who played because there was no one else. For Fowler, sadly the smiles were to be short-lived: his form vanished and Gooch and Robinson soon became England's established opening pair.

and the declaration came at 291 for two. The Australians then scored 39 more in an hour for the loss of Hilditch, their vice-captain, who is even shorter of runs than the England captain. He was caught at mid-off, trying to play through mid-wicket, for 21, but still managed to improve his average.

The two MCC openers missed out as well, having had to cope with the most difficult spell of bowling all day: Lawson and Thomson with the new ball. There is some truth in the theory that the nation is now awash with opening batsmen, but the trouble is that you can only play two at a time. In next week's one-day Internationals one is certain to be Gooch, but his first representative innings since the ban provided a reminder that his record against Australia is extremely ordinary. He was dropped by Wessels at second slip on 15 and did not add a run before Thomson yorked him.

Fowler, meanwhile, had his customary early trouble that suggests to bowlers that he is about to get out, and to those who know him best that he is about to score a century. This time the bowlers were right: he drove Lawson to mid-on on 24 just when he should have been set. Fowler has still not passed 50 this season and if he fails today it is hard to see how he can be in the one-day squad.

It is even harder to see how Nicholas can get in, given England's apparently padlocked middle order. But soon he may prise a means of entry. He was No. 5 on the card yesterday, but appeared first wicket down in place of Athey. At the time, with the quicks steaming in, Athey may have been grateful, although he will have become less so as the day wore on.

Some of Nicholas's early shots were improvised, to put it kindly, but as the bowling declined his innings developed authority and panache, especially through the onside. One or two people tried to make comparisons with Peter May; perhaps May himself did. One of his pulls had the dismissive assurance of Viv Richards. He is a player and captain of much promise, but he is competing for a Test place against players of proven achievement.

For instance there is Lamb, who scored his century, as ever, in the manner of a businessman dealing with the morning paper-work. It came quicker than Nicholas's - 166 minutes against 187 - but somehow it was less eye-catching. Lamb's batting so often seems mechanical, which is not a criticism – they said the same about Bradman. Lamb, like Nicholas, was strongest through mid-wicket; there was never any chance that he would not score a hundred.

The Australians had settled for a team with an extra bat but only four bowlers, and it told. Lawson, after his opening spell, appeared to be sparing himself; O'Donnell's medium pace looked a good deal less impressive than his batting; the left-arm finger-spinner Bennett, who has a nice, high action, was treated harshly when he gave the ball air and maybe concluded that English groundsmen are not as kind to him as the chap at Sydney.

Thomson was not flattered by his figures. He is bowling amazingly well. For personal reasons, I resent people being described as past it in their mid-30s, and so does he. He cut down his run after a while and bowled several of his slower balls, which are so slow that Underwood would disdain them. But for a long time he tore in, javelin action working. If Australia do not want him for the Tests, they can send him over to us – although the chairman of the selectors might want a word with him about his hair, which is now of a style and texture the like of which has not been seen since the days of Joe Brown and the Bruvvers and uncovered wickets at Old Trafford.

Thomson came off worse in his encounter with Nicholas than he did with another three-initialled county captain, the splendid John Robert Troutbeck Barclay of Sussex, who was struck in the mouth by him the other day. Through the pain, Barclay was heard to murmur: 'Is this the moment for heroics, or do we go off?' 'I'd eff off if I were you,' advised Thommo, not, I would guess, unkindly.

THIRD DAY

Lord's, Saturday 25 May

The news that the GLC regard Lord's as a fire-trap came through during one of the least inflammable days' cricket imaginable, with persistent drizzle cutting play by half and killing any chance of a result, grey clouds scudding across a dreary sky and the ground being enveloped by that air of damp lassitude that always signals a ruined match.

It was an extra pity, given the excellence of the batting on the first two days, and the enterprise of MCC's declaration on Thursday night. But the Australians were never in a position to respond and they batted out the last pointless hour, when the sun did come out and a few hundred people hung on without regard to their safety or the possibility of terminal boredom.

The selectors were thus able to head smartish up the M1 to commune with Gower and decide their 13-man squad for the one-day Internationals, to be announced tomorrow morning. Those special summer Sunday mornings, the lawn-mowing overshadowed by lists of names, some of them logical, are with us again.

We can assume they will begin with eight certainties: Gower himself, Gooch, Gatting, Lamb, Botham, Downton, Foster and Allott, leaving five places to be filled. They can always call anyone out of a county match if necessary, so there is no need to pick a spare wicketkeeper or anything.

The policy, one understands, will be loyalty to the men of India first, but I doubt if the selectors will be obsessive about it. Gooch is sure to open but his partner is more likely to be Robinson than, say, Larkins, and since a spare batsman will be required Fowler could easily be in as well despite his shortage of runs and confidence. There would be little point in including an extra middle-order bat like Nicholas, since he would be so unlikely to get a game.

My own feeling is that Robinson is a more natural foil to Gooch and the other current England batsmen than even an in-form Fowler. Supposedly, one-day cricket is not Robinson's strongpoint, but if he plays one of his calm, assured, just-ticking-along innings, he will allow the more effusive stroke-makers to take risks.

Fowler has done grand things for England, and it would be quite wrong to leave him out without a kind word and a promise of future consideration, but he is out of touch and Kim Barnett of Derbyshire might be a better bet as the extra opener. With the hunt for potential captains still on, the selectors might be particularly keen to give him an opportunity; for the same reason Gower might not.

There is a case for the inclusion of Willey as a No. 7 bat and

MCC v. AUSTRALIANS SCOREBOARD

AUSTRALIANS

A. M. J. Hilditch b Sidebottom	14	c Sidebottom b Williams	21
G. M. Wood lbw b Willey	33	c French b Gooch	48
K. C. Wessels c Gooch b Sidebottom	60		
A. R. Border b Underwood	125		
G. M. Ritchie c French b Williams	22	(4) b Athey	47
D. M. Wellham c French b Williams	0	(3) not out	81
S. P. O'Donnell not out	100		
R. B. Phillips not out	0	(5) not out	12
M. J. Bennett			
G. F. Lawson			
J. R. Thomson			
Extras (lb 8, nb 15)	23	(lb 2, nb 11)	13
Total for six declared	377	for three	222

Fall of wickets: 24, 117, 136, 164, 166, 372

Fall of wickets: 33, 117, 195

Bowling: Williams 17–2–74–2; Sidebottom 20–3–73–2; Underwood 27–4–93–1; Thomas 15.2–2–76–0; Willey 16–4–53–1

Bowling: Thomas 18–6–55–0; Williams 11–0–41–1; Underwood 4–3–3–0; Willey 4–0–14–0; Sidebottom 7–0–38–0; Gooch 16–2–46–1; Athey 9–0–23–1

MCC

G. A. Gooch b Thomson	15
G. Fowler c O'Donnell b Lawson	24
M. C. J. Nicholas not out	115
A. J. Lamb not out	122
C. W. J. Athey	
P. Willey	
A. Sidebottom	
B. N. French	
D. J. Thomas	
N. F. Williams	
D. L. Underwood	
Extras (b 4, lb 7, w 3, nb 1)	15
Total for two declared	291

Fall of wickets: 28, 52

Bowling: Lawson 17–1–66–1; Thomson 14–1–65–1; O'Donnell 14–3–77–0; Bennett 15–1–53–0; Hilditch 3–0–19–0

Umpires: J. Birkenshaw and A. G. T. Whitehead

Match Drawn

bits-and-pieces off-spinner, but the suspicion is that the selectors are leaning towards the inclusion of both Edmonds and Emburey as the best specialist slow bowlers in the country, with Emburey the more likely to play in view of Australia's preponderance of left-handers. That leaves one seam-bowling place, which could easily go to Cowans, despite the doubts about his effectiveness in one-day cricket.

He may be hard pressed by Sidebottom, although as a rank outsider Tim Tremlett of Hampshire is not an utter impossibility. Tremlett is about the most harmless-looking bowler in county cricket, which is part of his strength: the ball nips off the pitch far quicker than anyone suspects, and he is one of the most consistent wicket-takers in the game. His maiden century in the extraordinary Somerset-Hampshire match at Taunton this week will have done him no harm.

No one managed to add to the four hundreds at Lord's. The afternoon was wholly wrecked by the weather, although the players solemnly trooped out twice, once for 10 minutes and a second time for four balls. But after tea the clouds lifted and the players emerged to go through the motions. It was a waste of time for everyone except Wellham, who made his way to 81 not out against friendly bowling, his first decent score. Wellham is an adaptable cricketer who led New South Wales to Australia's one-day Cup earlier this year, and may well have forced his way into the one-day squad at No. 3. Oh, and Athey finally got a chance to do something: he was allowed a bowl and removed Hilditch's off-stump. He would rather have had a bat.

THE ONE-DAY INTERNATIONALS

Monday 27 May

For journalistic preference, it is always best on these Monday mornings to be able to regale you with some bright-eyed youth from the shires saying: 'I never had a clue till I heard it on the radio,' and: 'I didn't think the selectors knew who I was.'

That is not possible today. The England party for the three one-day Internationals against Australia is based on Peter May's belief that if selecting England cricket teams involves faith, hope and charity, the greatest of these is faith. The 13 chosen comprise 10 men who were in India, two rebels, Graham Gooch and Peter Willey, and Botham. The return of Gooch is a great moment for English cricket, but as a non-surprise it is matched only by the return of Botham.

Where there was a doubt, loyalty was the deciding factor. Thus both Fowler and Robinson are in as potential opening partners for Gooch, although there might have been a case for at least half-a-dozen others. It is unclear which of the two might get first crack, but the opening match, on Thursday, is at Fowler's home ground of Old Trafford, which may be significant.

Likewise, Cowans was given the one doubtful seam-bowling place. He is currently mixing brilliant spells (30 first-class wickets already this season) with dreadful ones in a manner that is un-predictable even by his own standards. This is easier for a captain to cope with in Tests than in one-dayers, and Cowans is the most likely person to be left out at Old Trafford, along with the loser between Fowler and Robinson. That would mean the inclusion of two spinners, with Peter Willey coming in at No. 7 and bowling his safe little off-breaks; though one of the many advantages of Gooch's return is that Gower will not be committed to 11 overs from anyone.

Willey scraped in ahead of Emburey, apparently on the say-so of his county captain, Gower. This was nothing to do with loyalty but a lot to do with depth of batting. Indeed, though Willey has many virtues, unquestioning fidelity to cricketing officialdom is certainly not amongst them. He was perhaps the most rebellious of all the rebels, almost certainly the one with fewest pangs. But his return is very welcome.

Willey left Northamptonshire after a bitter and very public dispute with the secretary, Ken Turner, who was militantly against the South African jaunt. The move to Leicestershire gave Willey's cricket more purpose, especially when Gower was away and he could assume responsibility, and also in matches against Northamptonshire, when he could vent his feelings by making stacks of runs.

It was clear last year that his jut-jawed courage and defiance were still mightily effective against fast bowling, and he could be a very inspired selection indeed. But at present he looks a short-term one. He is 35, never expected to last this long because of dodgy knees, and Emburey will almost certainly be chosen ahead of him for the Tests.

Like Gooch, Willey has a poor record against Australia (219 runs in 15 Test innings, compared to Gooch's 616 in 31), but the presence of both adds to the stature of an optimistic team. The selectors have almost an embarrassment of possible batsmen, the bowlers are in form, and Botham is in an astonishingly vibrant mood. His batting record in one-day Internationals, however, is very poor, largely because at No. 6 he only comes out for a slog or a crisis. He should bat at No. 5, or even 4; the great Botham feats of hitting come when he has time to assess the situation.

Botham returns to a mild caution from the chairman of selectors. Practice must be taken seriously. May said yesterday: 'The players must not only work harder. They must be seen to work at it.' In other words, Botham is not to spend his time in the nets taking aim at passing reporters. Quite so.

This correspondent, however, has faith both in Botham's essential good nature and in the overall quality of this team. It is the strongest England have chosen for many years, not just the three of the ban. The Australian attack has great power, but it is better adapted to Tests than to one-day games, and their batting order is as confused as England's is settled. Old Trafford will be followed by Edgbaston on Saturday and Lord's on Monday. A clean sweep is not impossible.

There remains the problem of Sir Donald Border. Only four batsmen have ever bettered his feat of four successive first-class centuries (Fry, Bradman, Procter and Weekes). One man, however, can give Gower a little reassurance: the chap who began the South African tour of 1956–57 with 68, 182, 118, 124 not out and 206, then averaged 15 in the Tests – Peter May.

Manchester, Thursday 30 May

In the sunshine at Old Trafford yesterday, the 13 men chosen for the three one-day Internationals against Australia assembled for the mundane business of nets. Today's opening match has the more elevated purpose of inaugurating a new era for English cricket.

Botham was back, hair bleached like Thomson (although there are rumours that Thommo has gone one jump ahead and dyed his grey) and wearing his caged-tiger look. Willey was there, looking strong and silent. And Gooch.

The whole of Lancashire wanted to shake Gooch's hand, and he responded in his best modest-hero manner. He tried to be just as stoic later when, as he was bowling in the nets, Lamb drove the ball straight at his rump. Then, when batting, he suffered the indignity of having his off stump removed by Gary Speak of the Lancashire Second XI.

The nets were not a great success. They were soft and slow after the rain earlier in the week, although the Australians had the worst of them when they tried to practise in the morning. The pitch for the match itself, though, appears dry and Gower thought it would turn. Almost certainly England will play both their spinners – Edmonds and Willey. Cowans's remarkable form and Fowler's home advantage suggest that Robinson and Foster are the players most likely to be omitted.

The batting order remains fluid and subject to what Gower calls his captain's whims. 'Sink or whim,' he announced breezily yesterday, suggesting that he may be feeling brighter about the world than he has done.

The most sensible whim, and an increasingly likely one, is the promotion of Botham to No. 4 or 5, where he will have more chance to turn the match. In 64 one-day Internationals he has a batting average of 20, and that is largely because he usually comes in so late.

The confrontation of the season will be between the Australian fast bowlers and the England batsmen. For the moment, the most fascinating point may be discovering which of the two astonishingly in-form batsmen, Botham and Border, can transfer their feats on to the greater stage. After Border's fourth century, at Derby on Saturday (which on some reckonings was the most brilliant of the lot), Geoff Miller said he was even harder to bowl at than Botham.

But the rest of the batsmen are still circling unsteadily around the captain in the order. Border himself reckons the bowlers are 'underdone', and the fielding has been patchy, as Lawson might fumingly testify. Cold hands should not be among the Australians' problems today. The Manchester weather is at its kindest. It should be quite an occasion – and quite a summer.

Manchester, Friday 31 May

The overture to the Ashes, the Texaco Trophy, began brilliantly at Old Trafford yesterday with a match which was absorbing throughout and thrilling at the finish. Australia won, which was a pity, but the occasion showed what mass-appeal spectator sport can be like on a good day and, in the North-west yesterday, hours after the tragedy in Brussels, that was a considerable public service.

With five balls to go, Greg Matthews struck the four the Australians needed to win by three wickets and go to Edgbaston tomorrow one up with two to play. Matthews had shared a stand of 34 with Geoff Lawson that just gave Australia the edge. But the contest for much of the day had resolved itself, in a manner so predictable as to be extraordinary, into a batting duel between the two men in prime form, Botham and Border.

Botham scored 72 against Border's 59 and took a wicket and

two catches to be named as man of the match by Brian Statham. But the later England batting, so capable on paper, proved less adaptable than the Australians'. England have now lost six successive one-day Internationals – in Australia, Sharjah and here – and there must be a tinge of worry to the springtime optimism surrounding the English game.

But it was a good day. There was very warm applause when Gooch and Fowler marched out to open for England. It was, I think, partly for the returned prodigal; partly for the local boy; partly for a gloriously clear day; and partly for the game itself, the fact that it is not soccer and they could expect to arrive home safely.

England, unsurprisingly, left out Robinson and Foster; the Australians left out Thomson (who may well have been detained by his barber overnight for observation) and played the leg-spinner, Holland, an indication of Border's growing pragmatism and of the dry, slow, bare-looking pitch.

But the Australian quicks soon broke through; Fowler was convicted of dangerous driving; Gower missed a slower delivery from Lawson that was almost an off-break; and Lamb was caught behind first ball. One had politely suggested that Botham might come in earlier, but the ninth over seemed to be overdoing it.

He emerged into the sunlight, bleached locks cascading from the back of his helmet. It was hard to say who he looked like, but it sure as hell was not Hobbs or Hutton.

The summer pudding of a pitch meant that everyone had trouble timing the ball. Gooch, after three years, discovered that he had come back to be, of all things, an anchor man. Botham, meanwhile, decided that if the ball was not going to come onto the bat he would leave the crease and fetch it.

He hit five sixes in the sector between straight and mid-wicket. It is, perhaps, Botham's destiny never quite to match his mate Viv no matter how he tries; and maybe he was conscious that this marked the first anniversary of Richards's own Old Trafford epic, 189 not out, the greatest one-day innings ever played.

This was not its equal, for quantity or quality, but it will do for most people. It ended, however, with him trying a reverse sweep against Matthews but missing and being bowled. It was not

Phil Edmonds bowling at Old Trafford.

the smartest stroke to play to an off-spinner on a turning pitch, and one specifically designed to bring out the bile in those cricket sages who prefer to observe the cracks in the Botham canvas rather than the masterful brushstrokes. When he bats like this, I think every one should be prepared to accept Botham's judgment. Statham seemed to take the same view.

Botham had beaten by seven his previous best in 64 Internationals and, presumably, his days at No. 6 in these games are over. But after Botham was out, the innings began to crumble, to Lawson and the batsmen's own inadequacies, and Gatting found himself without a partner.

Australia had 219 to chase. It was hard to assess their task on such a pitch, and their early batsmen, the W formation, had similar trouble to England, especially when the two spinners came on before tea, dropped on a length and tied the scoring rate down. When Willey bowled a rare full-toss, Wessels smacked it to straight mid-wicket and Botham, who also caught Boon, slogging, at short mid-on. Wayne Phillips joined Border and, with Australia's two best stroke-makers at the crease, the battle was really on.

With 11 overs to go, Border drove straight back to Allott and then Botham took out O'Donnell's middle stump. Australia needed a run a ball off the last 10 overs and it looked as though England might just have seized the initiative, but there was an eventful and, as it turned out, crucial over from Allott in which Phillips struck two fours and was dropped twice off difficult chances to Botham and Willey.

Five chances were missed in all, and Allott's mind may have gone back to the darkest days in India 81–82. But none of them was easy and they were all forgotten when Gatting took off at short third man and held on to a stinging cut from Phillips. Lawson emerged, having not batted at all on tour, and produced a cooler innings than several men who have had weeks of practice.

It was a grand contest all round, and if there was any idiocy from the 21,000 crowd, it came only from the men who sat shirtless in the sun all day and will be in red and puffy agony this morning.

The latest instalment in the adventures of Ian Botham took a new and strange turn last night when Peter May, the chairman of the England selectors, instructed Botham – and Gatting – not to play the reverse sweep, the shot that led to Botham's dismissal in the opening one-day International against Australia at Old Trafford on Thursday.

May said he had thumbed through the MCC coaching book and been unable to find the stroke. 'When you are an England batsman as strong and successful as they are, it's got to be an unnecessary risk.' It will therefore not be seen, from an England batsman at least, at Edgbaston today when the second game is played.

This presumably puts an end to the first battle in this summer's cricketing generation game between the critics and the criticised, although in a fairly extraordinary manner. The MCC coaching book was not written with one-day Internationals in mind.

You will probably be familiar with the Monty Python sketch in which northern businessmen compete with each other over their childhood deprivations – 'A shoe box? Lookshery! We lived in 'ole in the ground' – and there persists among former cricketers the feeling that their game belonged to a golden age of chivalry, competence and hardship. Everyone bowled a thousand overs a season of perfect line and length in borrowed boots, and did you hear them complain?

The dispute over the reverse sweep, condemned by almost everyone over 50, seems to crystallise the gap that exists between the former players and the current ones – idle, rich and unforgiveably young.

The shot was introduced to English cricket by Mushtaq Mohammed, and there are still only a handful of imitators. Javed is probably the most regular and most fluent user, Botham has always maintained that it is a safe shot. And if I added up all the reverse sweeps I had ever seen the score would be about 200 for 2.

The Old Trafford one-day International was dominated by the controversy over the reverse sweep. First Gatting tries it, successfully. Then Botham, disastrously. Next day Peter May removes it from their repertoire.

If played properly, it is a ground stroke to an unattended part of the field which is enchanting to the crowd and extremely unsettling for the bowler. The major problems are that the batsman virtually has to make up his mind in advance and if it goes wrong he looks a complete twit. There was some amusement in the bar on Thursday night at the thought of Peter Willey, with his mid-on stance, trying to play it. We concluded that it would probably require a crane to sort out the mess.

Now May has decided it is not a legitimate option. As the greatest postwar English strokeplayer he speaks with some authority, but I believe he has fallen for some of the absurdly overstated criticism of Botham. England lost on Thursday primarily because Nos. 7, 8 and 9 in the order – Willey, Downton and Edmonds – all failed to support Gatting in the closing stages. However, it is Botham's flash and swagger that diverts people. And now he is to be inhibited. It is very rum.

It may well be that Botham's determination not to be outdone by Gatting is not going to be an entirely healthy development for England. Already the smooth flow of authority from Gower and Gatting that contributed so much to the Indian success, seems to have come unstuck. With the field spread yesterday, England looked like the living embodiment of Bennite participatory democracy. And it is not merely Gower's captaincy on trial at Edgbaston today. He has six more innings for England to score the runs that would confirm him in the job. Everyone wants him to succeed; everyone knows he can. But the clock is starting to tick relentlessly.

Birmingham, Monday 3 June

Without regard to the dramatic needs of today's final match or our rocky national morale, the Australians won the second one-day International at Edgbaston on Saturday by four wickets, and with it the Texaco Trophy.

Much of the pattern was similar to the Old Trafford match on Thursday: England not quite scoring enough runs, not quite holding the catches that might have held back Australia, and Greg Matthews hitting the winning boundary, this time with six balls to go instead of five.

Botham at Edgbaston, in more conventionally aggressive manner.

This was a more brooding match, with a slow, agonising build-up, and there was nothing epic from Botham, but it highlighted the extraordinary contrast between the two captains: Border, who looks as if he could play the ball with a stick of rhubarb; and Gower, who looks as if he is doing just that.

Gower's seven-ball nought on Saturday, ending with a defeatist wave outside off-stump, was one side of the balance. In 14 one-day Internationals as captain he has made 271 runs – 154 in the last 10. Border's masterly match-winning (and man-of-the-match-winning) 85 not out was his seventh score of 50 or better in seven innings since he arrived here. The two men are friends and have immense mutual respect. In Australia in 1982–83, when Gower was the English crown prince, Border could not score a run. Border knows that neither man can go on this way indefinitely. Gower's head tells him the same. In his heart, though, he must be starting to wonder.

Gower is now like the prisoner in *The Pit and the Pendulum*. He has five innings before the end of the Lord's Test to find a way out of his dungeon of runlessness; Saturday's disaster was another very sharp turn of the ratchet. Except for a few air-heads in the crowd at Edgbaston, everyone wants him to escape. The selectors particularly must now be on the edge of their seats: they do not want to make Gatting captain if they can possibly avoid it.

The analogies with the last Australian tour in 1981 are mounting. Then, England also unexpectedly lost the one-day Internationals under the control of a captain whose form had mysteriously vanished. One fears that the ending may not be as deliriously happy for Gower as it was for Botham. Gower intends to bat No. 3 again at Lord's today, although he may be talked out of it by the selectors. 'Looking at it logically, I should bat three or I don't play,' he said. 'Gatt is probably the better of us going in later on, assuming we're both on form.

'If it's not three,' he added ruefully, 'it'll probably be nine.' There has been some criticism of Gower over this, but there were more grounds for it last year against the West Indies, when he could and should have shouldered the responsibility of batting three and instead sacrificed Randall and Terry.

Gower's own parting shot was particularly hideous (and should be the immediate subject of a banning order from Peter May, while he is in his determinist mood), but the pitch was stodgy and less comfortable for strokeplay than first impressions suggested, and Border was really the only batsman all day to play with perfect fluency.

Gooch batted magnificently, but this was not the Gooch of the past three years in county cricket, when he sometimes appeared to bat with one hand mentally tied behind his back, like a man playing beach cricket with his toddlers. His 115 was an innings mixing respect for the opposition with utter determination and remarkable concentration.

To settle the game, it needed someone at the other end to kick on, but both Lamb (23 overs for 25) and Botham had uncharacteristic difficulty with their timing. Border always thought that 231 would be gettable, and to make quite certain he did the important bit himself. When he reached 50 he raised his bat with the air of a man giving a routine greeting.

Afterwards he praised his players for their much-improved fielding, and announced that he would be lecturing them on the importance of going all out today and winning the series 3-0. This will be their 21st and last one-day International of 1985: then they can get on with the Tests, which the Australian players, if not their marketing men, still regard as the serious business.

Border's captaincy is growing in stature every day. It has an old-fashioned blood-and-guts quality to it, and he does not mind sounding a bit corny now and again. He mentioned the people who had labelled the team 'a second 17' and 'the worst ever to leave Australia', and was then asked if this was ever brought up in the dressing-room these days. 'Only when I want to get them going.'

Asked if he had any really pressing problems, Bob Merriman, the manager, replied: 'My putting.'

For the moment, the problems are with England. But it was another splendid day for the national game, as opposed to the team. The house was full, the drunks were friendly and the occasion was rounded off by the sight of David Shepherd, the rising star of the umpire's list, signalling leg-byes as though auditioning for the Tiller Girls.

David Shepherd, the former Gloucestershire batsman and the rising star of the umpires' list, who enlivened Edgbaston – both the one-day game and the Test – with his Tiller Girl signalling of leg-byes.

Lord's, Tuesday 4 June

Short of Peter May marching into their dressing-room and announcing that everyone's pay was to be doubled, it is hard to see how things could have gone better for England at Lord's yesterday.

They not only won the last of the three one-day Internationals against Australia, and won spectacularly – with eight wickets and six overs in hand – but did so largely through 102 from their captain David Gower, who has been widely obituarised these past few days.

Statistically, Gower was outshone by Graham Gooch, who scored his second successive century, 117 not out. But four days after his long-awaited comeback, Gooch has ceased to be news; we expect great things from him. Now we can once again expect great things of Gower, or at any rate hold out reasonable hope of getting them.

Well done, mate. Border congratulates Gower on the century at Lord's that ended his personal run famine.

Allan Border still received the Texaco Trophy on behalf of Australia, who had won the series at Old Trafford and Edgbaston; and Gooch and Border (289 and 188 runs respectively over the three matches) were the two men of the series. But Gower was not merely man of this particular match, he fundamentally altered the balance of power for the Ashes, which start at Headingley next week.

When he came to the crease the situation was decidedly unpromising. England were chasing 254 for five, the highest target of the series, and Robinson was out early. In the field there had again been ragged edges to Gower's captaincy and the odd dispute over field placings. Authority forgets a dying king. Much of the time he had stood at square leg with only Barrie Meyer to aid his thoughts. He emerged to bat looking somehow overwhelmed, like Paul Terry against the West Indians, or Androcles.

Gower was off the mark first ball and was applauded for that. Fortunately he resisted the temptation to acknowledge the crowd as Kim Hughes did, disastrously, at Melbourne in February. Then he was away; with a soundless flick off the hips for four, off-drives and pulls and sweeps, the footwork eventually assuming much of its old certainty. In one way it was reminiscent of Randall, whose best innings have always come when he had the least business to make them. But the shots were reminiscent of, well, Gower – and it was wonderful to watch.

It could all have been very different. He played and missed a few times then pulled Thomson for six to the Tavern, and Greg Ritchie got a hand to the ball on the wrong side of the rope. A few inches the other way and there might have been another sad trek back. But, in the short run, luck is everything in batting, and yesterday the luck was with Gower. It would be tempting now to say that his troubles are over. That could be as premature as some of the things that were said about him over the weekend.

It is still true that he would almost certainly make more runs for England this summer if he were not captain. But it is not the end for him and it might be a new beginning; it is certainly the end of the beginning of the end.

Gooch was more assertive than in his previous two innings, and oozed authority and sureness of touch. Together they put on 202 for the second wicket, the highest stand in any one-day Inter-

The captain and his biggest gun: Gower and Botham confer at Lord's.

national in this country. By tea it was clear that England would win, barring a major foul-up, and in the closing stages on another lovely, mellow day (contrary to established belief, God must like one-day cricket) the only doubt was who would reach a century first. The answer was Gower, and all Lord's rose to him.

One had sensed that the Australian total was vulnerable if England batted as they could. It was the easiest batting pitch of the series, and there were signs that perhaps Australia were not making the best possible use of it. Foster, included in place of Edmonds for reasons that remained mysterious but became irrelevant, had the new ball with Cowans, and they used it well. Wessels was injured, so Australia were without the first of their two focal points. And even Border played the odd false shot.

The first sign that yesterday might be different came when Border missed an attempted hook against Botham first ball. He made up for it soon enough with three crashing fours in an over off Allott, who has had a disappointing weekend. But Border missed a drive against Gooch on 44, the nearest thing he has had to a failure on the tour so far.

The major innings came from Wood, who took a liking to Lord's in the 1980 Centenary Test and made another century this time, 114 not out. It was in an innings of unexpected calm and sagacity, rather like Gooch's at Edgbaston, right down to the celebratory six after reaching three figures.

Wood did not even run anyone out until the final over, when it was inconsequential. And by then, with the help of 45 in 47 balls from the barrel-like Boon, Australia had upped their scoring rate considerably: eight an over from the last 10. But they could not possibly compete with what came later.

Afterwards, Gower expressed his gratitude to his team-mates and the crowds for their support during his bad run, which effectively dates back to the two centuries in Pakistan that earned him the captaincy. He did not mention the press.

Asked if he had contemplated giving up the captaincy, he said: 'I certainly wasn't going to give it up lightly. I think you could put this innings down to a bit of bloody-mindedness. It's pride in one's own ability and performance that matters in the end.' The result ends England's sequence of seven consecutive International defeats since leaving India.

ONE-DAY SCOREBOARDS

OLD TRAFFORD

ENGLAND

G. A. Gooch c O'Donnell b Holland	57
G. Fowler c Phillips b McDermott	10
D. I. Gower b Lawson	3
A. J. Lamb c Phillips b Lawson	0
I. T. Botham b Matthews	72
M. W. Gatting not out	31
P. Willey b Holland	12
P. R. Downton c Matthews b Lawson	11
P. H. Edmonds c Border b Lawson	0
P. J. W. Allot b McDermott	2
N. G. Cowans cb McDermott	1
Extras (b 2, lb 7, w 2, nb 9)	20
Total all out	219
54 overs	

Fall of wickets: 21, 27, 27, 143, 160, 181, 203, 203, 213, 219.

Bowling: Lawson 10–1–26–4; McDermott 11–0–46–3; O'Donnell 11–0–44–0; Matthews 11–1–45–1; Holland 11–2–49–2.

AUSTRALIA

G. M. Wood c Downton b Cowans	8
K. C. Wessels c Botham b Willey	39
D. M. Wellham cb Edmonds	12
A. R. Border cb Allott	59
D. C. Boon c Botham b Gooch	12
W. B. Phillips c Gatting b Cowans	28
S. P. O'Donnell b Botham	1
G. R. J. Matthews not out	29
G. F. Lawson not out	14
R. G. Holland	
C. J. McDermott	
Extras (b 2, lb 12, w 4)	18
Total for seven	220
54.1 overs	

Fall of wickets: 15, 52, 74, 118, 156, 157, 186.

Bowling: Cowans 10.1–1–44–2; Botham 11–2–41–1; Edmonds 11–2–33–1; Allott 11–0–47–1; Willey 9–1–31–1; Gooch 2–0–10–1.

Umpires: D. G. L. Evans and K. E. Palmer.

Australia won by three wickets

EDGBASTON

ENGLAND

G. A. Gooch b McDermott	115
R. T. Robinson cb O'Donnell	26
D. I. Gower c Phillips b O'Donnell	0
A. J. Lamb b Thomson	25
I. T. Botham c Wellham b Lawson	29
M. W. Gatting c Lawson b McDermott	6
P. Willey c Phillips b Lawson	0
P. R. Downton not out	16
P. H. Edmonds not out	6
P. J. W. Allott	
N. G. Cowans	
Extras (lb 2, w 2, nb 4)	8
Total for seven	231
55 overs	

Fall of wickets: 63, 69, 134, 193, 206, 208, 216.

Bowling: Lawson 11–0–53–2; McDermott 11–0–56–2; O'Donnell 11–2–32–2; Thomson 11–0–47–1; Matthews 10–0–38–0; Border 1–0–3–0.

AUSTRALIA

K. C. Wessels cb Willey	57
G. M. Wood lbw b Cowans	5
D. M. Wellham lbw b Botham	7
A. R. Border not out	85
D. C. Boon b Allott	13
W. B. Phillips c Gatting b Cowans	14
S. P. O'Donnell b Botham	28
G. R. J. Matthews not out	8
G. F. Lawson	
C. J. McDermott	
J. R. Thomson	
Extras (lb 13, w 2, nb 1)	16
Total for six	233
54 overs	

Fall of wickets: 10, 19, 116, 137, 157, 222.

Bowling: Botham 10–2–38–2; Cowans 11–2–42–2; Allott 10–1–40–1; Willey 11–1–38–1; Edmonds 10–0–48–0; Gooch 2–0–14–0.

Umpires: D. J. Constant and D. R. Shepherd.

Australia won by four wickets

AUSTRALIA		ENGLAND	
G. M. Wood not out	114	G. A. Gooch not out	117
A. M. J. Hilditch lbw b Foster	4	R. T. Robinson lbw b McDermott	7
G. M. Ritchie c Gooch b Botham	15	D. I. Gower c Border b McDermott	102
A. R. Border b Gooch	44	A. J. Lamb not out	9
D. C. Boon c Gower b Willey	45	I. T. Botham	
W. B. Phillips run out	10	M. W. Gatting	
S. P. O'Donnell not out	0	P. Willey	
G. R. J. Matthews		P. R. Downton	
G. F. Lawson		N. A. Foster	
C. J. McDermott		P. J. W. Allott	
J. R. Thomson		N. G. Cowans	
Extras (b 2, lb 13, w 6, nb 1)	22	Extras (b 2, lb 9, w 2, nb 9)	22
	—		—
Total for five	254	Total for two	257
55 overs		49 overs	

Fall of wickets: 6, 47, 143, 228, 252.

Fall of wickets: 25, 227.

Bowling: Cowans 8–2–22–0; Foster 11–0–53–1; Botham 8–1–27–1; Allott 7–1–45–0; Gooch 11–0–46–1; Willey 10–1–44–1.

Bowling: Lawson 9–0–37–0; McDermott 10–0–51–2; Thomson 8–1–50–0; O'Donnell 11–0–54–0; Matthews 10–0–49–0; Border 1–0–5–0.

Umpires: H. D. Bird and B. J. Meyer.

England won by eight wickets

FIRST TEST — HEADINGLEY

Monday 10 June

The England XII to start the assault on the Ashes at Headingley on Thursday has just one surprising omission, and that is hardly a shock to regular followers of selection policies. Phil Edmonds, lynchpin of the attack in India, has been dropped to permit the inclusion of two off-spinners, Willey and Emburey. Thus, from the one-day International squad Edmonds departs along with Fowler, while Emburey becomes the third ex-rebel to be recommissioned.

The bulk of the party was chosen with little discussion and will evoke little dissent. Everyone will be sorry to see Fowler go. It is both rough and rare for a player to be dropped two Tests after scoring a double hundred – Hardstaff in 1946 seems to be a precedent – but there can be no doubt that Fowler has lost form and not much more that Robinson is the better counterpoint to Gooch.

However, the mess over the spinners will cause controversy, although this time Edmonds's exclusion does not appear to be anything personal. No one has suggested that he has been sledging Thomson or trying to reverse sweep. Rather, the whole thing appears to be a classic committee botch, a compromise between the chairman of the selectors Peter May's understandable urge to include the best off-spinner in the country, Emburey, as a counter to Australia's profusion of left-handers, and Gower's urge to include his county vice-captain Willey as a back-up bat and bits-and-pieces bowler.

The greatest quality Willey will bring to the side is courage. He is the nearest thing English cricket now has to Brian Close. One hopes his attitude will infect the team. It would be even better if it could spread to the captain and selectors.

Quite likely, Edmonds's absence will not matter a jot this week. In the past 10 years spin bowlers have taken the grand total of 20 wickets in Leeds Tests. The last to make a significant impact was Edmonds himself, on his debut in 1975. And the Emburey theory is conventional enough, although Edmonds appears to be bowling the better of the two and if a slow bowler were to make a major contribution at Headingley, it would more likely be a left-armer turning the ball out of the rough near the left-hander's off-stump rather than anyone doing anything spectacular with off-breaks.

Well, all right. Edmonds would very likely have been 12th man anyway. Let us save our whinges until they try and leave him out of the Lord's Test. What is really depressing is the inclusion of Willey as the potential No. 7 – not because he is a bad player, though his indifferent record against Australian bowlers has not been enhanced by 12, nought and two so far this summer. There would almost certainly be no one better to turn to if the Australian pace bowlers gained the upper hand.

But here we are, the start of the series: Gower newly and gloriously refreshed by a run-transfusion; the Australian bowlers no-balling like crazy and as terrified of having to bowl down the Kirkstall Lane slope as the batsmen are of the pitch; England about to field what is beyond question – on paper – the strongest batting line-up in 20 years or more. And yet the first thought is defensive: leave out a class bowler and include another batsman – just in case. It is so wimpish.

There is one uncomfortable piece of history that may be relevant. In the opening Test of the 1968 series England played only three front-line bowlers, Snow, Higgs and Pocock, and had D'Oliveira and Knott at seven and eight, collapsed horribly twice (in these over-stuffed batting teams players seem to imagine they can safely leave things to the others), lost the Test and, effectively, their chance of reclaiming the Ashes from a much weaker side.

The selectors have some faith in Gooch's ability to swing the ball, and Foster may well be left out on Thursday. In that case Emburey, who made almost 800 runs for Middlesex in 1983, would be batting No. 9, which is great except that Cowans, Allott and Botham will be the only other frontline bowlers. Botham, apparently, had a dreadful time at Bath on Saturday.

One last thought on the batting: right now England could field a second team starting something like Fowler, Larkins, Tavare, Nicholas, one of the in-form Hampshire Smiths and Randall, that would compare quite respectably to some recent Test teams.

That is without mentioning, among others, either of the two Yorkshire openers, Boycott and Moxon. The sage Brearley wishes to include the senior of the two. But I can state with some degree of certainty that this can be ruled out utterly unless or until England go three down, Gower and May are carried out gibbering and either Brearley himself is brought back or the team's affairs are handed over to an extraordinary general meeting of the Yorkshire membership. By then, one trusts, Edmonds will have been given a game.

Leeds, Thursday 13 June

The Ashes series gets under way this morning, and as the participants gathered at Headingley yesterday the sun came out to greet them. It was only a trick, though: outside, something very close to a hurricane was lashing through Leeds, and if what the polar explorers call the wind-chill factor is the same this morning, the most eagerly-awaited Test for many years will get off to a pretty grim start.

The wind has helped dry out the pitch; it was in danger of starting very green. But the groundsman, Keith Boyce, is wearing his customary pre-Test look: as though he was waiting for the Home Secretary to ring up and reprieve him by calling off the match. The pitch will be the one used in 1981, the match lodged happily in every English cricketing mind except Boyce's. There is a relaid strip designed for Tests, but it is not yet considered trustworthy. No one trusts this one either, particularly not the Australians.

Boyce has worked immensely hard and talks of better root-growth binding the grass together and preventing the thing crumbling. It is said more in hope than certainty. But he deserves a bit of luck, and a Test that does not end in his crucifixion.

The magic phrase 'Headingley '81' has been on everyone's mind anyway. Five England players are here from the team that secured the impossible victory – Gower, Gooch, Gatting, Willey and, natch, Botham – and three of the beaten Australians: Border,

Lawson and Wood. That match is part of folk memory. For the Australians, so is the wicket; Wood came back here in the 1983 World Cup to face the West Indians on a flyer and was carted off to hospital after being hit by Holding. I think Australian mothers terrify their children by telling them Headingley will come up and bite them.

The '81 Test was not just a one-off. It began what has been a spectacular four years for English Test cricket – not, alas, in a playing sense, but certainly financially. Since then only one home Test in 19 has been spoiled by the weather, and all but four have produced results. Receipts have rocketed and public interest has probably never been higher. Today, for instance, only the unreserved seats are left.

Unfortunately, this confidence has not affected the playing side in the least. England's team selection for this match was essentially defensive, and it still seemed probable last night that they would play their seven batsmen and leave out a seamer.

The Australians were thinking along similar lines, although this was rather more understandable given their terror of this place and their fast bowlers' current problems. Lawson pronounced himself fit to play yesterday but he was still looking a bit peaky, and one suspects Border might be grateful if he can bat first and give his spearhead a little more time to get fit. The probability is that the Australians will play all their batsmen, with O'Donnell or Holland plus the three quicks. One gets the impression that both teams, as well as Boyce, would be happy to call this a draw and press on to Lord's.

Yet England should be full of beans. Gower, gloriously, is running into form just as Border, perhaps, is running out of it. One good innings here and Gower might be made captain for the summer. How are the stricken risen! And Australia's troubles could be increased by endless no-balls if the wind keeps blowing.

This series is most likely to be decided by the contest between England's batting and the Australian fast bowling, with Lawson, McDermott and Thomson as ace, jack and wild card. But there are six Tests and two well-matched teams, and it is unreasonable to try and predict what might happen. Anyone who did that successfully before the start in 1981 would have been locked up as a sorcerer. But England have immense batting talent and many advantages. Maybe what Gower needs most is something of Border's inspirational quality and belief. England have a wonderful opportunity to regain the Ashes; I hope they have the courage to make the most of it.

FIRST DAY

Leeds, Friday 14 June

The first phase of the first Cornhill battle at Headingley yesterday belonged to Australia, although not as emphatically as England had feared and perhaps deserved.

Just after tea Australia were 201 for two, with the vice-captain Andrew Hilditch on 119. Then he was out and his team finished the day at 284 for six. In the Test here in 1981 – the benchmark for this match and every other in which England are doing badly – the Australians scored 401 in the first innings before losing. There were moments yesterday when England appeared to be trying for the strategic follow-on.

Gone: Boon plays across a delivery from Gooch and loses a leg-before decision from Barrie Meyer as England fight back after tea on the first day.

This does not look a good pitch, although earlier it was hard to judge whether all the fears about it might be justified, because England bowled too poorly to give it a fair trial. They pulled round a little by performing much better towards the evening and by holding on to everything that went to hand. But the selectors chose a team to get a draw. They will certainly be content with that now.

So far, the game has belonged to Hilditch. You can never get away from comparisons with 1981 and people yesterday were recalling how Dyson made a scratchy 100 at the start of that contest. Hilditch looked as though he was going to do much the same, but his innings finished up as a very fine one: three hours to three figures, four hours in all.

When he first became Australian vice-captain from nowhere in the midst of the Packer schism, Hilditch became known as 'Andrew Who?' and until he came back triumphantly against the West Indies, it looked as though he would be remembered, if at all, as an Adelaide lawyer who got a few Tests in a very thin year.

Even six years on, he is not the most distinguished vice-captain in Australian Test history nor the most elegant player in the world. He has a low-slung stance, producing the bat late from behind the pads, as though he were trying to kid the bowler that he was unarmed.

But Hilditch gets his runs at the right time. Until last week, he was averaging less than 20 on tour and there was every chance that he would have been obliged to do the decent thing at the final selection meeting. He was saved by runs at Leicester and the decision to play an extra batsman. England must have thought he was the least of their problems. However, he comes good when it matters. Since his recall at Melbourne, he has scored 304 in four Test innings. And yesterday he reserved his false shots for the morning when Cowans and Botham were bowling too short to make them matter.

There were no surprises before the start. England left out Foster, Australia left out Holland and thus were without a serious spinner, and Gower lost the toss for the fifth Test running. Australia chose to bat first both because of their fears of what the wicket might become in the fourth innings and because of the doubts about Lawson's health.

It was a low-key start to the series all-round. The weather was still cold, although less blowy. The crowd was smaller than the advance sales suggested. And there was none of the spark of Ashes electricity that used to be generated whenever Lillee tore in. The handful of banners were all Australian ('Hello, Glen Waverley, Vic. Send more money, Glenn'). But it is going to be a long summer if not necessarily a long, hot one.

Perhaps eventually England will become more committed to winning. They went into this match with two trusty bowlers, Allott and Emburey, and two iffy ones, Cowans and Botham – plus Gooch (who was given more overs than any of them except, of course, Botham) and Willey, who has not yet bowled at all.

At one point there was a loud cry of 'Get A Proper Bowler' when Gooch trundled in. Headingley crowds always extend a warm welcome to Essex players, as Fletcher must have told him. It would have been more reassuring to see Foster or even Lever yesterday; they might have taken more advantage of the pitch's little perforations than anyone else. But Gooch shifted the ball around and took two important wickets, and the crowd became more friendly.

The only early success belonged to Allott who straightened one onto Wood's pads. The next couple of hours belonged to Hilditch and Wessels; it was a bit like watching a couple of crabs and England were obliged to have both a third man and a slash-stopper.

Free advertising on Kerry Packer's Channel 9.

In the end, one Wessels slash gave Botham a reaction-catch at slip. And just after tea and a 15-minute stoppage for bad light, Hilditch, apparently trying to take his bat away from a Gooch out-drifter, failed to do so, although his face suggested he thought otherwise.

Boon batted like a pools winner and, mercifully for England, Border was not at his best. They were out in successive overs, on 229: Boon having a horrid wipe, Border well held at second slip by Botham. Then there was a pleasing stand between the two fine stroke-makers, Ritchie and Phillips, which ended just before the close. Emburey, taken off immediately after dismissing Wessels, had Phillips very well held at silly point. The catcher was Gower, who celebrated by handing Botham the new ball.

Gower has been through a wide range of emotions in the last couple of weeks: despair at Edgbaston, elation at Lord's. Last night he might have been relieved that the situation was not far

---

First blood: Allott has Wood lbw for 23, the opening wicket of the Test series. It was the last for some time – Hilditch (with headband) went on to a century and put on 132 with Wessels for the next wicket.

worse. But the Australians, after a week of bowling troubles, with a decent total almost on the board and Lawson 24 hours nearer full fitness, have a great deal more to be pleased about.

SECOND DAY

Leeds, Saturday 15 June

The second day of the Headingley Test was a strange and bitty one, with half the play lost to rain and gloom. Yet the three hours' cricket that did take place was fascinating, and quite heartening for England. They bowled out Australia for 331, an above-par score for the pitch but one which England would have grabbed very gratefully at 201 for two or 326 for six. Then Robinson and Gatting led England to 134 for two. There will be no follow-on this time. And it is not yet impossible that England could win even without it.

Robinson was 66 not out at the close, having dominated the day almost as much as Hilditch did on Thursday. Both are under-rated cricketers who may well have an important influence on this entire series.

People have been underrating Robinson for a long while. When he came back from his successes in India there was much grey-beard muttering about how the quicks would find him out. Yet the people at Nottingham who know him best have said all along that he can play fast bowling; they were not sure before the tour how he might do against spin.

It was hardly a perfect innings yesterday. He began with an edged four and should have been caught by Ritchie at third slip on 22. But he proved several points, one of them being that he is not just a sticker. England have so far scored at five an over past the attacking field, and some of Robinson's back-foot strokes through the offside have been a delight.

One of Robinson's great advantages is that he is no fool. He has even managed to lose form this season without anyone having time to notice. Briefly, he began bending his leg, dropping his head and getting out. But he saw himself on the Trent Bridge video and, with help from his team-mate Hemmings, quickly sorted himself out. He also had the major asset yesterday of a below-par Australian attack. England have been so obsessed with their own worries before this game – hence the inclusion of Willey – that perhaps they have ignored Australia's deficiencies. Lawson, clearly still not totally healthy, had a wretched time and there was the predictable helping of no-balls, 11 in all.

But McDermott bowled very rapidly and very tenaciously and took both wickets: Gooch, perhaps burdened by the nation's expectations, was lbw and Gower caught behind to one slanting across him. Both balls shot through fast and low.

The last over of the day, O'Donnell's first in Test cricket, was quite something too. One English pro this season has called him a faster version of Pringle (this is considered a compliment round the circuit, if not among all spectators). O'Donnell can get bounce from unlikely surfaces: one delivery struck Robinson's glove, another Gatting's groin. It helped compensate O'Donnell for his first innings in Test cricket, which was the briefest possible. But the

Battle of the all-rounders: the Meyer finger goes up again (*below*) as O'Donnell's first ball in Test cricket ends with him being lbw to Botham. Four days later O'Donnell has his revenge and knocks Botham's off-stump out of the ground (*opposite*).

feeling persists that there are bowlers around who could cause mayhem on this pitch; none of them, however, are playing. Even so, as Gatting might have painfully reflected, batting was not all fun. And there were moments during the day when the whole match seemed joyless. As the rain came down, one felt that the whole four-year cycle of dry and bright home Test matches, which began with Headingley 1981, might somehow have been exorcised by the re-match. We had almost forgotten what a really damp and dreary Test was like.

There were five separate sessions yesterday, and two furious downpours. During the morning one Leeds city centre was said to be dry. There is a cloud over Headingley Test matches; the declining relative attendances have led to Yorkshire's being given the first Test – always considered the short straw – and to the long-term plan for Leeds to have a rota Test rather than an automatic one. But no one thought the cloud was quite so literal.

The Australian innings, proceeding very comfortably through the opening half-hour, was polished off very rapidly after the first stoppage. The last four wickets went down for five runs in 10 balls, a statistic which sounds a little better than it looked.

There was very nearly a Botham hat-trick: he dismissed Ritchie and O'Donnell in successive balls, and the next one only just whistled past Lawson's outside edge. However, it would have been a pretty rum hat-trick. Ritchie was actually bowled hooking, the ball managing to cannon down from the bottom edge. Then poor O'Donnell was lbw to his first ball in Test cricket.

Les Ames and Bob Wyatt, two of English cricket's senior citizens, will have greeted this with a sympathetic chuckle if they were listening: they started their Test careers just as badly. They might have been even more sympathetic if they were watching: the replays suggested the ball would have missed leg-stump.

Lawson, having narrowly survived his first ball, was plumb leg-before to the third, and Botham skidded one through on to McDermott's stumps next over to give himself three in four as a consolation. Botham wore his cat-got-the-cream look, and all his team-mates went in with a smile – although some wise heads thought the collapse might have helped Australia by saving time. There seemed, at this stage, something symbolic in the way the skies darkened as soon as the England openers walked out. Four balls later, it was raining.

However, the later play gave the day its flavour. And it was, all round, an improvement on the first. The crowd was bigger than on Thursday, when many people who had bought tickets evidently took fright at the cold and stayed at home. And earlycomers had the extra pleasure of seeing the England players do their morning contortions to the sound of the Hammonds Sauce Works Band playing Floral Dance. Nothing in the cricket could quite top that.

THIRD DAY

Leeds, Monday 17 June

There are days, and I think Thursday was one of them, when Leeds seems the ghastliest of all the cricketing cities: the Faisalabad of the North but with fewer functioning phone boxes.

There are other days, and these seem to happen whenever Australia are kind enough to turn up and act as stooges, when the place is touched by a unique magic, and English cricketers can make their wildest dreams come true. Saturday was like that: England improbably and gloriously took the first Test by the scruff of the neck; and in mid-afternoon, when Botham and Robinson were in, provided one hour of unforgettable batting ambrosia.

This morning England resume at 484 for 9, 153 ahead. For the first time in a home Test, David Gower held a Saturday-night press conference without being asked whether there was still a chance of saving the game. An England win is now the most likely of the three results. Australia will have to fight devilishly hard not to lose. They could win if they scored 300 odd, set England 130 and ... but, no, the Headingley magic does not work for them.

Actually, this match hardly seems to be taking place at Headingley at all. It might be happening in outer space. It is preposterous that 815 runs have been scored in 15 hours for only 19 wickets. Evidently, this surface slowed up on Saturday, while the sunshine stopped the ball swinging and further quickened the outfield; but the cracks in the area where bowlers should be pitching have not got any smaller. It is not the worst Headingley Test wicket, but it is not the greatest.

'It would be churlish to be critical of the pitch at this stage,' Gower said carefully, although his eyes said he was just as baffled

Afternoon delight: Botham (*opposite*) and Robinson (*above*) hit out in the golden hour of English batting on Saturday.

as everyone else. Border described Australia's bowling performance as the worst in years, and this gets somewhere near the nub. Lawson, who has told his captain that he is perfectly healthy, cannot possibly be; Thomson looked gone; McDermott and O'Donnell, in their third and first Tests respectively, were obliged to carry the attack. McDermott, a bowler of great promise, appears to have heart trouble, i.e. it is not big enough. And O'Donnell, who did very well in a quiet way to the ordinary batsmen, was cannon fodder to Botham.

Ah, Botham! He has been scoring a run a ball or better all season. The Jessop of the age. But that is strictly an average. He appears to have given up the routine business of running ones and twos except as an occasional concession to his partners.

He came out yesterday 40 minutes after lunch. Gatting and

Lamb had done their bit and departed. For the next hour Botham used his bat, the weight of an undersized new-born babe, instead of the traditional over-sized stick, like a machine gun. His 60 took 51 balls; but 52 of the runs came off only 12 of them.

There were the usual bellowing straight drives and hooks, but there were new tricks as well; on-drives and a delicious late cut. When Border brought himself on like an Anzac subaltern hurling himself uselessly at the Turkish lines, the temptation to reverse sweep must have been almost irresistible. Botham resisted, went for a conventional sweep and a huge straight six, and gave himself 50, and England the lead. You can stuff your nostalgia; Botham was brilliant.

We had almost forgotten that Robinson was still there. He kept his helmet on firmly while at the non-striker's end, since there was far more danger of being hit by Botham than by a bowler. 'Awesome,' Robinson said of Botham. But he was pretty awesome himself. Some of us who were in India have been trying to tell you what a good player Robinson is for quite a while.

Now you are going to believe us. He was scoring at a run every one-and-a-half balls, which is some going for a supposed anchor man, and he scored 175: the highest on an Ashes debut by anyone except R. E. Foster 81 years ago; the seventh highest England score against Australia since the war (behind Barrington, Boycott, Denness, Compton, Barber and Dexter) and 175 stabs to the vitals of Messrs Fowler, Broad, Moxon, Terry, Barnett, Benson, Larkins, Lloyd, Slack, and, since he still has delusions about the selectors' intentions, Boycott. The argument about openers has been closed.

Robinson said that he had kept going by adapting a lesson from his county colleague, Richard Hadlee. He continually set himself new targets to beat: first 100, then Hilditch's 119, then the 160 he had scored in Delhi. Robinson was just a Sheffield University sprog when the other Nottinghamshire lad, Randall, scored 174 in Melbourne, but he topped that too; then, mentally knackered, he edged Lawson to slip. He returned to the pavilion in the mellow evening sunlight, to be applauded by 20,000 contented Yorkshire souls (Robbo is a fan of Geoffrey's, after all) and patted on the head by Botham, who by now had changed into dark glasses and a black teeshirt and looked as if he was set for a bit part in the evening showing of *The Godfather*.

Well, Botham had batted rather like a god, and Robinson like a most dedicated apostle. The subsequent exegesis on their work by Willey, Downton and Emburey was worthy but an anti-climax. No one minded. The crowd had seen something very special.

FOURTH DAY

Leeds, Tuesday 18 June

Around teatime yesterday the bowlers and the Headingley pitch finally began working in harness and, thanks to a little burst of wickets from John Emburey, England were able to sight victory in the First Test. Provided the weather stays kind and the remaining Australian batsmen do not have unsuspected reserves of determination, they should land some time this afternoon.

At the end of the fourth day, Australia were 190 for five, still 12 runs behind. England lost 35 late minutes of wicket-taking time to the light. It seemed only middling bad, but the Australians thought they got a raw deal when Robinson and Gatting were allowed to go off on Friday (and Border said so very strongly to the umpires); maybe they were trying to be even-handed. It was a

Poor Lamb: bowled by O'Donnell for 38 in the first innings.

shame for Peter Willey, though – he was finally about to be allowed a bowl.

The rest of the unhappiness belonged almost entirely to the Australians. In the morning they had humiliation piled on top of indignity when Downton and Cowans put on 49 for the last wicket, and took the England total to 533 and the lead to 202. This was England's highest-ever score against Australia at Headingley and their highest anywhere against them since The Oval in 1975, 29 Tests ago.

It was an extraordinary passage of play, dominated by the Downton hook and the Cowans shove. The 500 came up with a most contemptuous pulled four by Cowans off poor, broken Thomson. It was like watching the last hoodlum in the gang kneeing the dying victim in the groin before running away.

Life immediately got even worse for Australia, and especially for Wood, who had been off the field suffering from back spasms, which were not bad enough to stop him whirling into a Botham bouncer/long-hop (delete to taste) which Lamb, one of the two long legs set for the purpose, took brilliantly – the classic sucker-punch.

This brought together Australia's two best stickers, Hilditch and Wessels. They stuck there and kept scoring in a stand of 139 at four an over. This match has largely belonged to the marginal choices, Hilditch and Robinson, and Hilditch almost managed to steal back the honours. He was out 20 short of becoming the first Australian in almost 40 years to score two centuries in an Ashes Test. It was another secure, controlled innings.

It was not flawless, though. Robinson dropped one very hard chance. And, since not much was happening for England at this stage, two otherwise insignificant balls assumed greater importance. They may or may not have come off the bat – probably not – but they incontrovertibly spilled out of Downton's gloves.

It was lucky that he had again showed what a determined run-getter he can be, because the long-standing doubts about Downton's wicketkeeping began to turn into a general rhubarb. He does look vulnerable at present, especially on the rare occasions for England when he finds himself standing up. As yet, no one can agree on an alternative. That may not persist indefinitely unless he recaptures his old form.

But England's failure to break through cannot be blamed on Downton. The pattern of the match was holding, with the batsmen in control to a bewildering extent. Then Emburey switched to bowl up the slope from the Football Stand end. Almost at once, one kept low and Wessels, the one Australian player you could envisage batting for two days, was bowled off his pads.

Then, after tea, Hilditch swept to backward square leg; Border was surprised by lift from Botham, caught behind for eight and thus failed totally for the first time all tour; and Ritchie was bowled by a delivery from Emburey that shot through, as the Australians say, like a Bondi tram, and almost tunnelled under the off-stump. From 144 for one, Australia were 160 for five.

Botham's wicket was his 110th against Australia, putting him ahead of Wilfred Rhodes, in 24 Tests against 41, and behind only Willis. But there were no more successes. Phillips and Boon held on as the clouds became darker. If they do not portend anything too wet today, England should triumph, and no one will bother about the side issues like wicket-keeping. The players will be feted in a way not seen since . . . well, the last time they played Australia here. And, who knows, one effect might be that both sides will start playing spin bowlers in the Tests ahead.

FIFTH DAY

Leeds, Wednesday 19 June

England beat Australia in the First Test at Headingley yesterday, although they were forced to fight harder than expected throughout the final day. There were only 13 overs left when they settled the match by five wickets.

The day also belonged to what the England captain David Gower called 'a pack of mad dogs' as well as all other Englishmen. The winning runs came from a skyer hit by Allan Lamb, which Geoff Lawson dropped after the traditional post-match stampede had begun.

One youth was only a few feet from Lawson while he was trying to take the catch en route to a scrummage to try to grab the stumps as souvenirs. The Australian captain, Allan Border, declined to complain – 'It was a difficult catch anyway,' he said –

but Gower and Peter Lush, the Test and County Cricket Board spokesman, called the incident disgraceful and Lush said that talks would be held before the second Test at Lords a week tomorrow in an effort to prevent a repetition. He added: 'The crowd behaviour throughout the rest of this game was excellent. Cricket's very good record must be protected, but a solution is extraordinarily difficult.'

Cricket seems unlikely to produce a Brussels. But this incident is not unique: Terry Alderman, the Australian fast bowler, was seriously hurt rugby-tackling an invading spectator at Perth in 1982; Michael Holding was injured when the crowd rushed on to Lord's after the 1983 World Cup final. The Oval Test last year was close to anarchy throughout.

England go to Lord's one up, with five to play. Since 1905 whenever they have won the first Test at home to Australia, they have failed to win the series.

The 170th anniversary of the Battle of Waterloo was marked yesterday by another famous victory over an equally traditional enemy. When the battlefield cleared – and in view of the crowd's performance, that turned into a more exact metaphor than anticipated – England had won the first Test by five wickets, their third successive victory at Headingley over the Australians; poor Allan Border would probably rather they play on St Helena in future.

It was not even a damn close-run thing, although it was a great deal closer than England had expected or imagined. They needed 123 to win, and every last run had to be eked out grudgingly from the bowlers and the pitch; this was five days old yesterday and entitled to be a bit crabby, but it had never been up to generally-recognised Test standards, and it is hard to imagine that any team has scored more than England's 533 on a worse one. That innings was the basis of England's triumph, and the chief architect, Tim Robinson, was rightly man of the match.

This is a triumphant moment for England and David Gower. The unit forged in India and reinforced by the returned exiles has done everything that could have been expected of it. But the captain himself failed again yesterday, caught at second slip for five, after 17 in the first innings. Gower was only made captain for two

Phillips ducks a Botham bouncer.

Tests, because of doubts over his batting form rather than his leadership. It would be right now to take the heat off and extend his term at least to the third Test (though Peter May, the chairman of selectors, was not even present yesterday to consider that option) but it may still be premature to look further ahead than that.

Thanks to the fatheads who ran on before the winning runs were secure, even the result was not entirely untainted. And, almost to the end, it was possible to make fanciful comparisons with Headingley '81: Australia then, chasing 130, were 58 for one and 111 all out; England yesterday, needing seven fewer, found themselves 83 for four, with the highly promising O'Donnell bowling particularly well.

Even past the point when the joke bowlers might normally have appeared, O'Donnell was still steaming in, and there were 12 successive balls without a run off the bat. The Australians had not given up when Lawson tried to get underneath Lamb's skyer, only to find he had about 500 rivals charging on to try and grab the stumps. They have certainly not given up the Ashes yet either. There are five Tests to go.

As far as the crowd goes, cricket is not yet football, and they can hardly ban us from Europe. But it might be best not to be smug; as the Oval Test last year also showed, there is a desperate need for extra policing on these final days of Tests, when the crowd is smaller, but more agitated. We ought not to be smug about the cricket either. The Australians will surely not bowl as badly again when Lawson is fully healthy, and they have realised that no matter how redundant a spinner looks on Thursday morning, it is a different story on Tuesday afternoon. Australia were one up before their disasters in 1981 as well.

This was supposed to be so simple for England. Australia were still 12 behind at the start with five out. Boon was bowled off his boot by the sixth delivery of the day, and the new ball was imminent. But O'Donnell and, more particularly, Phillips refused to go quietly. They not only hung around, but complicated both ends of the equation by scoring rapidly as well.

Phillips is a lovely touch player and some days it is a pleasure to watch him. But this was not one of them for a partisan, and especially not for the England fielders; apart from the considera-

The beginning of the end: Thomson hails what would have been his 200th Test wicket, but his captain Border puts down a straightforward chance at mid-wicket. Lamb looks on anxiously.

tion of winning, seven of them are engaged in today's Cup semi-finals and they were anxious to be down the M1. At first the stand seemed irrelevant, then mildly niggling; then horrible imaginings started, worsened by some dark, brooding clouds. Finally, O'Donnell and Phillips, who made 91, gave catches off Botham; and Emburey, who finished with five for 82, did the rest. England had 200 minutes to get the runs, heaps of time, and Robinson and Gooch quickly put on 44.

But there was trouble ahead. Robinson was bowled through the gate; Gower hit one crisp four past square leg before giving a catch to second slip; Gooch was beaten by an O'Donnell nip-backer, and Gatting went to a diving catch behind. Botham's first ball struck his pad and Lawson, fooled by umpire Palmer's elaborate flick of the pebble from one hand to the other, was con-

The bitter end: Lamb's speculative legside blow that finishes the match . . . Lawson gets into position to catch but the crowd have already decided the game is over . . . and head for the middle to try and grab the stumps as souvenirs. In the wake of the Brussels soccer tragedy, this incident makes even cricket crowd behaviour front-page news.

England v. Australia

AT HEADINGLEY

First Test Match

Thursday, Friday, Saturday, Monday & Tuesday, 13th, 14th, 15th, 17th & 18th June, 1985

ENGLAND WON BY 5 WICKETS

ENGLAND

First Innings:		Second Innings:	
1—G. A. Gooch lbw McDermott	5	lbw O'Donnell	28
2—R. T. Robinson c Boon b Lawson	175	b Lawson	21
*3—D. I. Gower c Phillips b McDermott	17	c Border b O'Donnell	5
4—M. W. Gatting c Hilditch b McDermott	53	c Phillips b Lawson	12
5—A. J. Lamb b O'Donnell	38	not out	31
6—I. T. Botham b Thomson	60	b O'Donnell	12
7—P. Willey c Hilditch b Lawson	36	not out	3
†8—P. R. Downton c Border b McDermott	54		
9—J. E. Emburey b Lawson	21		
10—P. J. W. Allott c Boon b Thomson	12		
11—N. G. Cowans not out	22		
Extras	40	Extras	11
Total	533	Total (for 5 wkts.)	123

FALL OF WICKETS :

First Innings : 1—14 2—50 3—186 4—264 5—344 6—417 7—422 8—462 9—484

Second Innings: 1—44 2—59 3—71 4—83 5—110 6— 7— 8— 9—

Bowlers	Overs	Mdns.	Runs	Wkts.	Bowlers	Overs	Mdns.	Runs	Wkts.
McDermott	32	2	134	4	McDermott	4	0	20	0
O'Donnell	27	8	77	1	Lawson	16	4	51	2
Lawson	26	0	117	3	O'Donnell	15.4	5	37	3
Thomson	34	3	166	2	Thomson	3	0	8	0
Border	3	0	16	0					
Wessels	3	2	2	0					

NOTE : Wides and No-Balls are now debited against the bowler

* Denotes Captain   † Denotes Wicket Keeper

Umpires : B. J. Meyer and K. E. Palmer

Scorers : E. I. Lester and M. P. Ringham

AUSTRALIA

First Innings:		Second Innings:	
1—G. M. Wood lbw Allott	14	c Lamb b Botham	3
2—A. M. J. Hilditch c Downton b Gooch	119	c Robinson b Emburey	80
3—K. C. Wessels c Botham b Emburey	36	b Emburey	64
*4—A. R. Border c Botham b Cowans	32	c Downton b Botham	8
5—G. M. Ritchie b Botham	46	b Emburey	1
6—D. C. Boon lbw Gooch	14	b Cowans	22
†7—W. B. Phillips c Gower b Emburey	30	c Lamb b Botham	91
8—G. F. Lawson c Downton b Allott	0	c Downton b Emburey	15
9—C. J. McDermott b Botham	18	c Gooch b Emburey	6
10—S. P. O'Donnell lbw Botham	0	c Downton b Botham	24
11—J. R. Thomson not out	4	not out	2
Extras	18	Extras	8
Total	331	Total	324

FALL OF WICKETS :

First Innings : 1—23 2—155 3—201 4—229 5—229 6—284 7—326 8—326 9—327

Second Innings : 1—5 2—144 3—151 4—159 5—160 6—192 7—272 8—307 9—318

Bowlers	Overs	Mdns.	Runs	Wkts.	Bowlers	Overs	Mdns.	Runs	Wkts.
Cowans	20	4	78	1	Botham	33	7	107	4
Allott	20	3	74	2	Allott	17	4	57	0
Botham	29.1	8	86	3	Emburey	43.4	14	82	5
Gooch	21	4	57	2	Cowans	13	2	50	1
Emburey	6	1	23	2	Gooch	9	3	21	0

NOTE : Wides and No-Balls are now debited against the bowler

Hours of Play : Thursday to Monday, 11.00 a.m. to 6.00 p.m.

Tuesday, 11.00 a.m. to 5.30 p.m. or 6.00 p.m.

Lunch : 1.00 p.m. to 1.40 p.m.

Tea : 3.40 p.m. to 4.00 p.m.

ADJUDICATOR : CORNHILL Player of the Match — R. G. D. WILLIS

Player of the Match — R. T. Robinson

vinced his appeal was about to work, and was most upset when he realised it was not.

From then on, Australia's path was downward, although O'Donnell did remove Botham's off-stump. Really, Australia did not deserve to get Botham out. Lawson started bowling at him with a long-on and a long-off, field placings which were based on a caricature of his approach. I cannot recall Botham ever holing out in the first over, certainly not in a Test. It would have made far more sense to post extra slips.

The Australians refused to give in, and Thomson thought he had his 200th Test wicket when Willey gave a simple chance to mid-wicket. Border put it down. He might now have a moral obligation to keep Thomson in the team. The England selectors may soon feel a similar obligation about Gower.

SECOND TEST — LORD'S

Monday, 24 June

The England selectors, in their wisdom, yesterday announced two changes in the 12 for the Lord's Test on Thursday. In addition to the expected and welcome recall of Phil Edmonds in place of Peter Willey, Norman Cowans has been dropped in favour of Arnie Sidebottom, the uncapped Yorkshire seamer. The selectors apparently intend to play two spinners plus Neil Foster, 12th man at Headingley, which means the final place rests between Sidebottom and Paul Allott.

Peter May, the chairman of the selectors, said that while it was tempting to keep a winning team together, it would have been wrong not to change the attack after its erratic performance last week. 'We would not have been true to ourselves,' May said. 'It is hard luck on Cowans, but we were concerned about his control. Sidebottom is a bowler who has been quietly getting on with his job, and he can bat a bit.'

That bland statement may conceal a wonderfully inspired piece of committee work. Sidebottom marked his inclusion with a far-from-quiet celebratory rattle of wickets at Harrogate yesterday. Perhaps it needs a Yorkshireman for England to beat Australia at Lord's: the last win was Verity's Test of 1934. There are, however, several reasons for thinking it may not quite work out that way for Sidebottom.

To start with the good news, the return of Edmonds means that the two best slow bowlers in the country will be operating together for England for only the second time. On the only previous occasion, at Lord's seven years ago, they were virtually redundant: Botham and Willis bowled out New Zealand for 67. But a well-balanced England team needs both Edmonds and Emburey. And it is not easy to see this week's pace attack doing anything similar to Australia.

One had always supposed that the point of picking 12 was to leave as many options as possible open for Thursday, when it might be possible to have a clue about the nature of the pitch. The selectors appear to have left themselves no option at all but to choose between Sidebottom and Allott, who are similar sorts of bowlers. And if they don't know which one they prefer now, it is hard to see how they will know any better on Thursday.

Sidebottom for Cowans is also an unusual variant of the horses for courses principle. Playing the Middlesex man at Leeds and the Yorkshireman at Lord's seems a bit like running a Grand National horse at Royal Ascot and vice versa. (Incidentally, Foster hates Lord's. His only two Tests in England have been there, and he was dropped after each; the last time after Greenidge had flogged him into adjoining suburbs.) What might matter more is that a 24-year-old has been replaced by a 31-year-old; a bowler with 38 first-class wickets this year by one with 17; and a man with sufficient pace to match Lawson and McDermott by a typically England fast-medium seam and outswing type.

Cowans has no divine right to play for England. Heaven knows he is unreliable and the selectors might well think that, westward, the land is brighter with Lawrence of Gloucestershire and Thomas of Glamorgan (both locally born) starting to cause fast mayhem from previously unconsidered directions. But Cowans is capable of deliveries, overs, and even spells of world class speed and hostility. England have rejected him, without knowing the pace of the Lord's pitch, in favour of an attack that might, if things go badly, bear a horrible resemblance to the troupe of medium pacers humiliated by Pakistan at Lord's three years ago, the first time Gower was left in charge.

Sidebottom may add a little solidity. Since giving up football four years ago (having declined from Manchester United to Halifax Town) and becoming the last and apparently least well paid of Gooch's South African rebels (he did not even play a first-class match on the tour) he has improved steadily as a bowler and a worker. Last year he finally acquired the confidence to take the new ball for Yorkshire; before then he used to find, curiously, that the shine caused it to slip through his fingers.

Although there has always been the suspicion that he suffers from a touch of the Chris Olds (owing to the odd strain and the curiosity of Yorkshire's fixture list, he has hardly played any cricket for three weeks), the feeling in Yorkshire is that he will have no trouble standing up to a five-day Test. And, as May says, he can bat.

One up in the series, Australia in disarray, England's best stroke-making line-up in years in prime form, and one of the reasons for dropping the main strike bowler is to strengthen the batting. You want to weep sometimes, really you do.

Lord's, Thursday 27 June

Even the weather retreats when faced with the might of MCC. Colonel John Stephenson, one of the club's assistant secretaries, stood in the middle of Lord's in his wellies yesterday morning and evidently commanded the rain to cease.

For a few precious hours Lord's was bathed in sunshine and the wicket for today's second Test was allowed to see daylight. The forecast, for what that is worth, suggests that cricket's remarkable run of luck may hold. In this winter among summers, we have so far managed three sun-drenched one-day Internationals and an excellent Test match, although the county season has endured two months of purgatory. The ground staff will bust a gut to start the match on time this morning, and are expected to work all night with the 'whale' machine. They would do so anyway, even if it were not for the new deal whereby spectators get their money back if there is no play and officialdom gets even more frantic about the weather than in the old hard-cheese-if-it-pours days.

But a week with more than three inches of rain has taken its toll on Lord's and the new groundsman Micky Hunt: the outfield yesterday was like one of the wetlands that are supposedly a threatened habitat in southern England: the pitch has had only a third of its normal rolling; and part of the rest of the square, covered by tarpaulins for the last few days, is under attack from the dreaded fuserium fungus, an old enemy from wet summers past. It will not affect this match but, if the worst comes to the worst, there could be some odd pitches at Lord's later this season.

The wicket will almost certainly be soft and slow today, and both teams were gearing up to place greater reliance on spin than at Leeds. England are expected to play both Edmonds and Emburey, with Sidebottom now the favourite to miss out; Australia have named 12, including both the leg-spinner Holland and the slow left-armer Bennett, but not Jeff Thomson, so they will have to play one slow bowler at least.

One is tempted to feel a bit sorry for Australia. They have followed their Headingley disaster with a miserable and, by all accounts, bad-tempered performance at Southampton. Logic would suggest that if three uncapped Hampshire bowlers can get the Australians out for 76, then the might of England should do rather better.

However, history may be a better guide than logic. This is the 21st Lord's Test against Australia this century. So far England have won just one (1934) and lost seven (1909, 21, 30, 48, 56, 61 and 72), very often on the occasions when the Australians have been most disdained. The sight of all those MCC members seems to bring out the Aussie fighting streak better than anything else.

The soggy ground prevented anyone using the Lord's nets yesterday. Australia headed for the indoor school at Finchley. England settled for a team talk instead. David Gower was trying hard to regard this as just another Test match. But his term of office as captain ends on Tuesday, and there is no word yet about an extension. The selectors are in a bit of a corner. It would be most unjust to replace Gower at this stage, especially now that so much of the old pizazz has returned to his batting. I doubt if they would wish to do so or could agree on a successor.

If England win and Gower makes runs, there can hardly be a problem. But a personal failure by Gower in the context of an England success may pose a particular difficulty. At Headingley there was a happy four-year-old memory of Botham. Here there is the one of him a fortnight earlier, out for a pair and getting his retaliation in first by resigning before he was sacked.

Large numbers of stewards and police will be on guard to prevent a repetition of the invasion at the end of last week's Test. It would be nice if Gower was not expected to endure a repeat of another unpleasant bit of history. He does not deserve it.

FIRST DAY

Lord's, Friday 28 June

The opening day of the Lord's Test provided a personal success
for David Gower, who made the runs the selectors told him to
make and can now expect to be England captain again at Trent
Bridge two weeks hence.

However, the general picture is more disconcerting for Gower.
None of his team-mates passed 50, and England finished at 273
for eight. Everyone knew that Gower could bat. How he handles
the next four days may provide far more significant evidence about
his fitness to keep the job in the long term.

It was not an entirely satisfactory day for Australia either. They
put England in, but seemed to take the wickets almost in spite of
themselves. One of Sir Thomas Beecham's bon mots (of more
universal application than 'Have you ever played Stockhausen?'
'No, but I once trod in some') was 'Whatever you do, do it with
conviction,' and Allan Border might think about that. If you're
going to field first voluntarily in a Test match, you really have to
believe that you can bowl the opposition out. Australia once again
had only four bowlers: Lawson, supposedly their best, began with
a third man despite the dead outfield; and Holland bowled to
Gower without a single close fielder to cater for the possibility
that the ball might turn.

Luckily for Australia, Gower's charges also did not play with
much conviction. Certain traditions were observed. Gatting was
lbw padding up in his third consecutive Lord's Test; Botham, in
his fourth innings here in Tests against Australia, took his grand
total from nought to five; and the reliable situation-savers Downton and Emburey later prevented an utter collapse.

If there was a genuine hero, it can only be Micky Hunt, the
groundsman. No one who squelched round Lord's yesterday seriously believed that play could start on time, yet not a second's
play was lost.

There was actually half an hour extra, mainly because Lawson,
who was no-balled 21 times, appeared to be waging a one-man
campaign to bring back the eight-ball over. It was a triumph of
spike and sponge.

At the start, when Jack Bailey, the MCC secretary, read out a message appealing for spectators to be considerate – which was code for Trespassers will be Executed – the thought was that 24 hours earlier this would have been unnecessary. Anyone running on the outfield could easily have drowned.

England left out Sidebottom and so in the end probably had their best possible team for the conditions. Australia, more dubiously, kept out Bennett. Then Gower lost the toss for the sixth Test running. The sequence began when he stopped his sequence of losing, so perhaps it doesn't matter.

The softness underfoot gave everyone problems. The bowlers had trouble with the run-ups and, in contrast to Leeds, only the best shots reached the boundary. Gower got there 12 times.

In the morning, England lost Robinson and Gooch, both lbw to McDermott, and both times there was some muttering about umpire Evans's decision, although the replays were inconclusive.

The age of elegance is back: Gower's first-innings 86 secured his future as captain.

Gooch was just getting close to full flow. Gatting's disaster came two overs after lunch, and Lamb made a very patchy start.

However, Gower was batting about as handsomely as anyone could on such a slow pitch. One square-driven four was probably worth an extra Test as captain on its own. Otherwise, his grandest strokes came off the back foot, and his last, fatal drive, edged to second slip after three and a quarter hours and 86 runs, was the first time his footwork had faltered. Gower has never made the centuries he should have done, but this could easily have been his third against the Australians inside a month. Beyond question, no one in cricket habitually makes better 80s.

Australia's successes largely came just before or after intervals. Tea separated Gower's dismissal and Botham's overexuberant miscue to deep point. Lamb, having grafted to 47, was caught behind, driving, an hour later. Emburey, in his rooted way, played worthily until he was lbw (no arguments) in the final over.

But it had all gone a bit flat after Gower was out. Somehow the occasion of the St John's Wood year has not yet quite lived up to its billing. If the ball still seams around today, Foster and Allott may provide a more interesting challenge than Lawson and McDermott managed yesterday. And maybe the ground will be fuller. After the unprecedented scramble for advance tickets, so many people were put off that some of the unreserved seats remained unsold.

SECOND DAY

Lord's, Saturday 29 June

The forecast had promised sun early and rain later, which at least would have been clear-cut. Instead, the weather was grey all day, and much of the cricket in the second Test yesterday also fell into grey, disputatious areas. Not for the first time a full house left Lord's feeling vaguely dissatisfied.

Even the position is a mess. When bad light halted play for the fifth and last time at 5.50, Australia were 183 for four, 107 behind England, and had evidently acquired a small advantage, having been in trouble at 101 for four when Greg Ritchie joined his captain, Allan Border. Border is now 92 not out.

Both captains can now feel personally chuffed, but both must also feel like anglers wrestling with a large but slippery fish; control of this game is eluding them. A draw may well be the proper outcome, but that is likely to require more determined batting and worse weather than has been evident so far.

Yesterday had far more right to be a full day than Thursday. The ground had dried out considerably, and the pitch as well as the outfield had quickened up. But 70 minutes were lost overall to the light, and the extra hour came nominally into play, although no cricket took place.

It usually looked that, of the two umpires, David Evans was marginally less keen to play than Dickie Bird. This was understandable: Evans has had a troubled two days, with a lot of difficult decisions to make. Not everyone is pleased with the way he made them.

Umpire David Evans in what might have been the uneasiest moment of a difficult Test match.

Evans is a most improbable villain. He is a Welshman, and a gent, and a philosopher – and a good umpire too. But he is making fallible, human, high-pressure instant decisions, which are then reassessed at leisure in front of a million television sets. Quite likely, he should not have given Gooch out lbw on the first day; very possibly, he should have given Wessels out caught behind on two but not, as he did, lbw for 11. Wessels was given the slow death, which means Evans took a few seconds to make up his mind. Umpteen replays later, it was possible to conclude that the ball may have pitched outside leg stump, and might conceivably have been too high. But only the most dogmatic souls could be quite certain Evans was wrong.

The light was a different matter. The playing regulations for the series state that 'the umpires will only suspend ... play for bad light when they consider that there is a risk of serious physical injury to the batsmen.' You need a fairly optimistic view of England's attacking potential to consider there was such a risk on every occasion yesterday. The Australians thought they had the rough end of the umpiring at Leeds, both over light and dismissals. Perhaps, the umpires might just have been trying to be extra fair to the Australians over the light. The regulations imply that fairness to the customers should be a bigger factor.

It was, all in all, unsatisfactory cricket for a day when the Queen came along and a British male won a match at Wimbledon. Even Ritchie's strokeplay, some of which was luscious, could not persuade Her Majesty to hang on long after she had been presented to the teams. (She appeared to speak most meaningfully to the two ex-South Africans, Lamb and Wessels, but this must have been coincidence.) And the crowd had pushed off long before the umpires had announced officially that there would be no more play.

England, who had started the day on 273 for eight, added 17 more between breaks. McDermott took the two remaining wickets – Foster caught at gully, Edmonds at second slip – and finished with six for 70 to become the latest in the long line of young Australians whose Test careers have taken a quantum leap at Lord's. He will probably bowl better and fare worse, but there is no doubt that Australia have unearthed a cricketer who could be an important influence on the game way into the 1990s.

Matthews meets the Queen, with Wellham next in line. Border looks on anxiously: spirited young Australians have been known to make less than deferential remarks on these occasions.

England's bowlers were soon on their way, too. Wood, whose form has gone, had a horrible swing at Allott and was caught at long leg. (Allott has now taken seven Test wickets against Australia, and four of them are Wood.) Hilditch, dropped at second slip by Botham on seven, only doubled his score before he drove at Foster and had his off-stump untimely ripped.

McDermott on his way to six for 70 at Lord's: 'the latest in the long line of young Australians whose Test careers have taken a quantum leap at Lord's'.

Wessels scratched around for 90 minutes over 11 before Evans gave him out; the decision was certainly justifiable on grounds of quality control. Then Boon gloved an excellent Botham bouncer to give a catch behind just before tea: the Queen met a happy England and a subdued Australia.

But Border was still batting, and in that mood of utter control that he had in the early county games; his driving was particularly splendid. But when he reached 87 – supposedly Australia's un-lucky number – he touched off yet another argument by giving Gatting a catch at forward short-leg which had three separate stages. First it went between Gatting's thighs, then into his hands, then upwards and on to the ground while Gatting dived forward to try unsuccessfully to retrieve it.

Had Gatting thrown it up in triumph, or like a hot brick? Was the dive an instinctive act or the despairing move of a man who knew he had blown it? Umpire Bird had no doubt that Gatting did not have the necessary 'complete control over the further disposal of the ball', and gave Border not out. Botham, most obviously, disagreed. No one could blame Evans this time. And the crowd were most agitated at this stage by the under-bowling of Emburey; you could not blame Evans for that either.

THIRD DAY

Lord's, Monday 1 July

One of the problems of reporting cricket is the extent to which the game takes place on a level above logic. How can one sensibly explain why, tour after tour, and no matter how awfully they have been playing, the Australians come to Lord's and make England look like Charlies? How can one explain the way in which Botham, with a supposedly injured ankle, galvanised the England attack on Saturday after his four colleagues, all better-equipped technically, had failed to make any impact at all?

It would be extremely harsh to blame David Gower, who last year was criticised so much for overbowling Botham, for neglecting him now. But it does seem that Gower, whose own cricket can be so gloriously fey and instinctive, does not have that extra mystical dimension as a captain.

He also has a disconcerting tendency to try and lead from the back. On Saturday night not only did Gower opt for two night-watchmen rather than risk himself, he was also a bit bewildered by questioning on the subject. He thought it was obvious why he had saved his best batsmen for Monday. The idea of facing the music himself did not appeal to him as a strategy or even register as a possible symbol of England's intention to fight back.

On any level England are, undeniably, in a mess. They start the fourth day of the second Cornhill Test this morning on 37 for two, 98 behind Australia. Both openers have gone, and the likely effect of the dual night-watchman policy is that Emburey and

Allott, two men who might have been very helpful as aides to whoever emerges to lead the English resistance, will not be available.

Gower's Saturday night reading of the pitch certainly seemed
more in tune with reality than Border's. Border talked about turn
for bowlers from the Nursery End, movement off the seam at the
other, and said that he would not fancy chasing more than 150 –
which could easily be what Australia do have to chase – in the
fourth innings. Gower does not consider the wicket itself a problem. 'The job still has to be done. It is capable of being done.
There are class players left capable of saving this match.' But the
force is with Border at the moment. He has just scored 196. If he
thinks he made it on a minefield, it's a minefield.

The match was turned by his fifth wicket stand of 216 with
Greg Ritchie who made 94. Until Botham, blood up, appeared in
mid-afternoon, hardly anything daunted them. Border is a high-
class batsman in the pink of form. He is a bit like a left-handed
Lamb: essentially orthodox, but when he hits, he hits mighty hard.
The extra seems to be his masterly judgment of length, which
enables him to be in the right place at the right time to play the

Australia's Saturday: The stand of 216 between Border and Ritchie for the fifth
wicket turned the match. Border's command was absolute; Ritchie's strength-
through-joy strokeplay was a delight.

right shot. This was a superb innings, although in many ways Ritchie's was the more interesting.

One of the seminal moments of Border's captaincy is reckoned to have come in the early days of this tour in the Lord's nets, when Ritchie chose what he thought was a quiet moment for a quick cigarette. Border suddenly rounded on him like the put-that-light-out ARP warden in Dad's Army. No one had ever seen Border exert that kind of authority before, and it changed several players' perception of him as a leader.

Now, 100 yards away, the two of them put together a partnership that may well have transformed the series and the tour. At 101 for four with every chance of going 2–0 down, the whole Australian campaign was in danger of disaster. Now 1–1 looks very possible.

Border may well get much of the credit for Ritchie's play, aside from cutting down his smoking. Ritchie didn't play against England in 82–83, having lost his place because of Greg Chappell's return, and then got a bit fed up, both with selectors and people telling him that he was doing it all wrong. Border has told him to play his natural game, loft the ball if he feels he can get away with it, and ignore anyone with inhibiting advice.

Ritchie lives in the coal town of Ipswich, outside Brisbane, a couple of miles away from McDermott. The pair of them have provided the continuation of the classic pattern: the brash young colonials coming to Lord's and punching the Poms on the nose. Eventually, no doubt, they will return as honorary members and tell anyone who will listen that the next generation is useless.

Botham also reacts well to Lord's, and Saturdays, and large crowds. And he carried England's bowling for his 25th set of five wickets in an innings. Whatever has been said about his belly in the past, there is fire in it at the moment.

It seemed as though England had retrieved the situation a bit: Australia's lead cut down to 135, Gooch and Robinson in no apparent difficulties, the match looking highly saveable for England. Then McDermott surprised Gooch off the pitch, and Holland beat Robinson in the air, and the England dressing-room was filled with the sound of hasty buckling and unbuckling of pads.

There is enough time and English talent for this match to have any number of twists yet. But at present an Australian victory is

An important miss: Allott, trying to cope with the sun, drops O'Donnell after a top-edged hook against Botham. O'Donnell went on to make 48.

the most credible possibility, even allowing for further illogic, and not catering for the chance that Lawson might finally emerge from mediocrity and bowl at his brilliant best.

FOURTH DAY

Lord's, Tuesday 2 July

At the end of the fourth day last night, Australia looked like winning the second Test, which was precisely the situation at the

Robinson is bowled by Holland late on Saturday, the wicket that led to the double-nightwatchman incident. The Australians, remembering Headingley, are rather pleased.

start of it. That bare, but inescapable, fact conceals an absolutely breathtaking day's cricket, dominated by the Somerset Samson, who gave England hope where none should rightfully have existed.

For a real believer, that hope still exists this morning. Australia, needing 127 to win, spent 21 overs making 46 of them, lost three wickets on the way and had the holy terrors whenever Botham went near the ball. Border's strange prediction that 150 would be a hard total to chase on what still looks to outside eyes a straightforward wicket may yet turn into a self-fulfilling prophecy. Botham's contribution was 85 runs and two wickets, the second of which was number 326 in Tests, taking him past Bob Willis's England record and behind only Lillee in the world. But his whole play had the mark of a biblical champion smiting primitive tribesmen.

Unfortunately for England, they have done a few primitive things themselves. The double-nightwatchman policy proved every bit as disastrous as the wise men prophesied, putting England in the psychologically traumatic position of 57 for four in less than 40 minutes and forcing Botham and Gatting, who turned into his faithful cohort, to bat without a safety net. In particular, England were deprived of Emburey, who could have been a far more significant figure against the tired bowlers of the afternoon than was ever plausible against the fresh men and newish ball of the morning.

England, 135 behind on first innings and 37 for two overnight, were all out for 261, the leg-spinner Holland taking five for 68. Half the score, 130, came in the stand between Gatting, batting at six ('too low' – P B H May, after the one-dayers) and Botham at eight. Gatting batted for more than four hours, after coming close to repeating his lbw padding-up trick first ball, and was left stranded on 75. While the stand was on, an extraordinarily full Monday house could suspend its grip on the reality portrayed by the scoreboard. At times Lord's had the atmosphere of a one-day final – in the nicest possible way.

They came together 40 minutes before lunch. Lawson had done for Allott – fourth ball of the day – and Emburey. Gower, briefly, batted like a dream: five fours (one more than Gatting), including three in a row off Lawson, one of them a peach of an off-drive. If today holds, among other things, the sacking of Gower as captain, it cannot be because his batting confidence has gone. But the dream was only part of a catnap. On 22, he again tried to drive. The delivery was from McDermott but similar to the one from Lawson that Gower had despatched so beautifully. This time the feet stayed still and the ball found the edge. Seventy-seven for five. Then Lamb sent Lawson's slower ball straight to mid-off. Ninety-eight, or minus 37, for six.

Botham came out to join Gatting. The precedent in older minds was Lord's 1953 when Bailey and Watson engineered one of English cricket's most famous Dunkirks. But you know Botham. His policy at Dunkirk would have been to try and march on Berlin. He was prepared to make a circumspect start, though, and there were no fireworks until the over after lunch, when he hooked McDermott into the Mound Stand. Botham was especially careful against Holland. It was a weird tableau: a grey-haired leg-spinner from the Nursery End bowling to our bare-headed hero, while fielders in baggy green caps hovered and an airship progressed serenely over Regent's Park. At tea one half-expected the teams to be presented to George V.

For much of the time Holland bowled round the wicket looking for the rough, which enabled Botham to play him in perfect safety with the pad. But when he used his bat, he used it like a warclub: in 13 overs after lunch, he raced from 23 to 74, playing just about every shot, and playing them all con brio. There was a hard chance to Hilditch in the covers on 41, but otherwise Botham just demoralised the Australians, until he jabbed his bat hard down against his toe. When hit by that great thing even the Botham toe feels it.

He batted on after treatment, and the Australians were beginning to run out of options. McDermott was warned a second time for running on the pitch and so, like a motorist with two endorsements, became scared of speeding. Remembering Leeds, Border was afraid to bowl O'Donnell at Botham. Holland was kept on, out of necessity rather than courage. But it paid off. Finally Botham aimed for long-on, found only Border at cover-point and departed, livid. The next ball from Holland hit the rough, the shoulder of Downton's bat and the grateful hands of slip. Edmonds, after 50 minutes and a single, cut to slip. Foster went second ball. And the applause for Gatting's second-highest Test score in England was drowned by that for gentle, 38-year-old Holland.

Gower had to give Botham the new ball. He charged in, bad ankle, bad toe, bad times forgotten. Hilditch obliged him fourth ball by a daft hook into the two-man trap. Then Botham beat Wood with extra bounce, and the catch lobbed to gully. Nine for two, and Willis's record had gone.

Ritchie, promoted because Border had been hit on the ankle, tried to force Allott, who deserved some luck, and was bowled. Now Border was obliged to come out and, together with Wessels, hung on to the end. On Sunday Botham and Border were playing golf together. This whole match has hung on the interplay between them. And surely only Botham can possibly stop Border now.

FIFTH DAY

Lord's, Wednesday 3 July

Ninety minutes after the start of the final day of the second Test, David Gower trudged off the field at Lord's with the rest of the England team, defeated, but relieved by his personal sweetener from the selectors; an hour earlier it had been announced that he would be captain for the remaining four Tests this summer. Next stop: Trent Bridge a week tomorrow.

In every other respect, the day belonged to the Australian captain Allan Border. His side reached their target of 127 with four wickets standing to square the series at 1–1. And once again it was Border who personally steered the innings away from the rocks with 41 not out. He took Australia to victory, passed 5,000 runs in Tests, was named Man of the Match, and conclusively settled this round in his private war with Botham. Asked how he planned to celebrate, Border replied his wife was arriving soon.

The Australians now have three free days to savour the victory. For Gower, even the good news of his reinstatement may seem a bit negative. One of the best features of Peter May's term as chairman has been the absence of unnecessary captaincy crises; taking Gower to the brink before reappointing him was uncharacteristic. The decision to give him all four Tests rather than just one or two was more in keeping. The impression is that the deciding factor was the Thatcherite principle, There Is No Alternative. There has been considerable Establishment dissatisfaction over several aspects of Gower's tactics and approach, but the only plausible rival is Gatting. And the case for him – if Peter May accepts it, which I doubt – is insufficiently compelling to justify a sacking in mid-series.

They are right to persist with Gower, but the nagging feeling remains that a grand cricketer is being just a little miscast.

It could easily have been 2–0 to England, which would have made a sacking even less possible. The daft anti-Aussie joke is that they are well balanced people, having a chip on each shoulder. The chips they carried yesterday were marked Headingley and Edgbaston '81. And at 65 for five, once again, the Australians were fearing the worst.

Gower's brilliant reflex throw from silly point that runs out Wessels and has Australia worried at 63 for four.

They had resumed at 46 for three, but, somehow Botham could not quite recapture the fervour of Monday in the last-morning calm, and Edmonds began to emerge as the major threat, bowling into the rough created by McDermott's quasi-legal follow-through. The first wicket was a bit of a fluke. Wessels was the victim of a brilliant run-out, almost a stumping, from Gower at silly point. But then Edmonds turned one a mile out of the foot-marks, past Boon's backward defensive on to the off stump, and all Australia went quiet.

Border was still going, though, and he was joined by Wayne Phillips, allegedly a nervous character, but determined not to show it. Phillips decided to get on the back foot and attack by square-cutting. There was one cut too many in the end, and Edmonds

The celebrations: McDermott, Boon, Lawson, Ritchie (with customary cigarette), Border and Holland.

took a splendid catch. But by then Australia were only 11 short of victory, although they never felt safe until O'Donnell, on Border's advice, went down the track to Edmonds and hit him for six over the top.

In the closing stages Australia's worst problem came when Jack Bailey, the MCC secretary, chose 116 for six to make his plea for the crowd not to run on at the end, to Border's considerable annoyance.

The plea worked, though. At the end everyone behaved as if it were the end of evensong in a particularly overpowering cathedral, eventually filing towards the pavilion for the presentations in dead silence broken only by the traditional victory chant coming from the visitors' dressing-room: 'Australia, you effing beauty!'

All good friends: Botham and umpire Bird walk off when the Test finishes (*above*); vanquished Gower and victorious Border smile on the Lord's balcony (*opposite*). Gower has the consolation of keeping the captaincy for the series.

One sensed through all this that somehow the will was not there for an England win, either in the team or across the nation. At 1-1 it can hardly fail to carry on being a great series; at 2-0 the Ashes might have been pretty secure for England, but dramatic necessity dictates that Australia do not fall apart just yet.

England need not panic. They are probably only one strike bowler away from having a very good team indeed. One would guess they will try Cowans in that role at Nottingham, but if he fails then the Gloucester tearaway David Lawrence may appear sooner rather than later. Against that, Australia have squared the series without much of a contribution from Geoff Lawson. He must strike soon.

The later cricket in this match more than compensated for the messiness at the start and a few unhappy umpiring decisions. Border, with a winner's insouciance, yesterday rejected any idea of electronic aids. 'Human error is part and parcel of the game,' he said.

LORD'S  GROUND

CORNHILL INSURANCE TEST SERIES
ENGLAND v. AUSTRALIA

Thurs., Fri., Sat., Mon. & Tues., June 27, 28, 29 & July 1, 2, 1985 (5-day Match)

ENGLAND

			First Innings		Second Innings	
1	G. A. Gooch	Essex	l b w b McDermott	30	c Phillips b McDermott	17
2	R. T. Robinson	Nottinghamshire	l b w b McDermott	6	b Holland	12
†3	D. I. Gower	Leicestershire	c Border b McDermott	86	c Phillips b McDermott	22
4	M. W. Gatting	Middlesex	l b w b Lawson	14	not out	75
5	A. J. Lamb	Northamptonshire	c Phillips b Lawson	47	c Holland b Lawson	9
6	I. T. Botham	Somerset	c Ritchie b Lawson	5	c Border b Holland	85
*7	P. R. Downton	Middlesex	c Wessels b McDermott	21	c Boon b Holland	0
8	J. E. Emburey	Middlesex	l b w b O'Donnell	33	b Lawson	20
9	P. H. Edmonds	Middlesex	c Border b McDermott	21	c Boon b Holland	1
10	N. A. Foster	Essex	c Wessels b McDermott	3	c Border b Holland	0
11	P. J. W. Allott	Lancashire	not out	1	b Lawson	0
			B 1, l-b 4, w 1, n-b 17,	23	B 1, l-b 12, w 4, n-b 3,	20
			Total	290	Total	261

FALL OF THE WICKETS

1—26	2—51	3—99	4—179	5—184	6—211	7—241	8—273	9—283	10—290
1—32	2—34	3—38	4—57	5—77	6—98	7—229	8—229	9—261	10—261

ANALYSIS OF BOWLING

Name	1st Innings						2nd Innings					
	O.	M.	R.	W.	Wd	N-b	O.	M.	R.	W.	Wd.	N-b
Lawson	25	2	91	3	...	15	23	0	86	3	...	1
McDermott	29.2	5	70	6	...	2	20	2	84	2	4	2
O'Donnell	22	3	82	1	1	...	5	0	10	0	...	...
Holland	23	6	42	0	...	...	32	12	68	5	...	...

AUSTRALIA

			First Innings		Second Innings	
1	A. M. J. Hilditch	S. Australia	b Foster	14	c Lamb b Botham	0
2	G. M. Wood	Western Australia	c Emburey b Allott	8	c Lamb b Botham	6
3	K. C. Wessels	Queensland	l b w b Botham	11	run out	28
†4	A. R. Border	Queensland	c Gooch b Botham	196	not out	41
5	D. C. Boon	Tasmania	c Downton b Botham	4	b Edmonds	1
6	G. M. Ritchie	Queensland	l b w b Botham	94	b Allott	2
*7	W. B. Phillips	South Australia	c Edmonds b Botham	21	c Edmonds b Emburey	29
8	S. P. O'Donnell	Victoria	c Lamb b Edmonds	48	not out	9
9	G. F. Lawson	New South Wales	not out	5		
10	C. J. McDermott	Queensland	run out	9		
11	R. G. Holland	New South Wales	b Edmonds	0		
			B , l-b 10, w 1, n-b 4,	15	B , l-b 11, w , n-b ,	11
			Total	425	Total	127

FALL OF THE WICKETS

1—11	2—24	3—80	4—101	5—317	6—347	7—398	8—414	9—425	10—425
1—0	2—9	3—22	4—63	5—65	6—116	7—	8—	9—	10—

ANALYSIS OF BOWLING

Name	1st Innings						2nd Innings					
	O.	M.	R.	W.	Wd.	N-b	O.	M.	R.	W.	Wd.	N-b
Foster	23	1	83	1	1	...	...	...	...	...	...	...
Allott	30	4	70	1	...	...	7	4	8	1	...	...
Botham	24	2	109	5	...	4	15	0	49	2	...	...
Edmonds	25.4	5	85	2	...	...	16	5	35	1	...	...
Gooch	3	1	11	0	...	...	...	...	...	...	...	...
Emburey	19	3	57	0	...	...	8	4	24	1	...	...

Umpires—H. D. Bird & D. G. L. Evans   Scorers—E. Solomon & M. P. Ringham

† Captain   * Wicket-keeper

Play begins each day at 11.00

Luncheon Interval 1.00—1.40

Tea Interval 3.40—4.00 (may be varied according to state of game)

Stumps drawn at 6.00, or after 90 overs have been bowled, whichever is the later. (In the event of play being suspended for any reason for one hour or more in aggregate on any of the first four days, play may be extended to 7.00 on that day). The captains may agree to stop play at 5.30 on the 5th day if there is no prospect of a result.

Australia won the toss and elected to field

Australia won by 4 wickets

THIRD TEST — TRENT BRIDGE

Monday, 8 July

The England selectors yesterday responded to defeat at Lord's by dropping the 12th man, Arnie Sidebottom, and bringing in the 25-year-old Leicestershire fast bowler, Jonathan Agnew, for the third Test at Trent Bridge on Thursday.

Once again there is likely to be widespread bewilderment, not least in the Sidebottom household. It is, after all, as if a company chairman reacted to a fall in profits by firing the tea boy. But it seems to me that England may have chosen their best-designed squad for some while.

Sidebottom is unlikely to see it that way, poor thing. There can be few disappointments in sport quite as stark as making an England 12 without ever becoming a Test player. In the past two years it has happened to Dave Thomas, of Surrey, and (through injury) to Sidebottom's Yorkshire team-mate, Martyn Moxon. At the Oval in 1971, the Somerset opener, Roy Virgin, was left out on the Thursday morning, and for him the call never did come.

There is nothing Sidebottom can do except keep bowling his heart out and instruct his garage not to add the words '... and England' to the side of his sponsored car just yet.

But taking a wider perspective, it looks as though the selectors have moved in the right direction by including a bowler of genuine speed for use on a pitch that might turn out to be pacey, and picking a 12 that leaves them a decent number of options. Any one of the bowlers, except of course Botham, could be left out, although Allott appears to be the ante-post favourite. I gather the selectors are anxious to give Foster another chance, but would like him to concentrate on swinging the ball instead of trying too hard to bowl quickly.

Arnie Sidebottom: in (at Lord's originally); out (on the morning of the match); out again (when the Trent Bridge team was chosen); in (when Foster withdrew); and out (when he hobbled off).

Agnew can be quick and of late has been proving it. He has taken 33 wickets this summer at 26 each (well behind Cowans) but he was injured throughout May. In all competitions in June, only Malcolm Marshall took more wickets. After discussion of John Lever, the choice is believed to have narrowed to Agnew and Cowans, with the eventual decision being made on immediate form. It obviously does Leicestershire players no harm to have Gower as England captain.

It is still not easy to see Agnew as a Test spearhead in opposition to Lawson and McDermott. If Cowans is a bowler of occasionally devastating spells, then Agnew is a bowler of occasionally devastating deliveries. He is capable of what the pros call a 'Jaffa' (the one that tucked up Greenidge in the Oval Test last year might have been the ball of the series) but the Jaffas all too often come in a barrel of rotting Golden Delicious.

The Australians will not mind his inclusion. Agnew was a complete failure in the one-day World Championship there this winter (nought for 59 in eight overs against Australia in Melbourne) and conceded 144 in 26 overs in the tourist match at Leicester last month. But he is improving – this season he has been habitually pitching the ball nearer the batsmen's end – and he is acquiring more experience. Until he was picked against the West Indies last summer, his biggest match had been a NatWest quarter-final at Northampton. His inclusion is a risk: life is rarely dull when Agnew is bowling, and I would take a small wager that Cowans will reappear somewhere before the series is through. But until ready-made Larwoods and Truemans start crawling out of the pits again, it is the sort of risk England selectors have to take.

The rest of the team, happily, almost picked itself, and Robinson got nicely into trim for his first home-ground Test with a century on Saturday. Peter May is believed to be anxious for Gower to be protected a little from the new ball by moving down to number four, with Gatting at three, although the choice is to be left to the captain. One can only note that the one lengthy recent period when England did not have a number three crisis has been when Gower did the job. Perhaps it might be psychologically valuable if the position were abolished and, in the manner of houses being numbered as 12a, the batsman in first wicket down could be called number four, and the last man number 12. I am sure the Australians would be very understanding.

Paul Allott: in bats beaten, outswingers applauded, batsmen outglared, umpires intimidated and appeals rejected, he probably led the field. Unfortunately he did not take enough wickets for the selectors' taste.

The England selectors were obliged to rearrange their thoughts on the fast bowling for tomorrow's third Test when Neil Foster withdrew from the squad yesterday because of a back strain. Arnie Sidebottom, who by now must be very confused indeed, was hastily rerouted from Maidstone to Trent Bridge to replace him in the 12 which convenes for nets this afternoon.

Any injury to Foster's back, which has given considerable employment to the medical profession, must give cause for concern, but he insisted yesterday that this was only a strain. He hopes to be fit to play for Essex again by the weekend, but felt he had no chance of being right by tomorrow, so his strange record continues: he has played only three home Tests, all at Lord's, and has not yet done himself justice in any of them.

Sidebottom, dropped after being 12th man at Lord's, where he presumably did an unsatisfactory job as drinks waiter, must again be favourite to be left out; an opening attack of Agnew and Sidebottom, with two Tests and none respectively, would place even more weight than usual on Botham. However, the selectors are believed to be a little concerned about Allott's effectiveness, and with the current inconsistencies over fast bowling policy, anything is possible.

At Gloucester over the weekend, Sidebottom was plagued by no-ball troubles, which suggests that his ups and downs over the past three weeks have inspired him to try harder rather than give up. However, he looked very ordinary indeed – as did the whole Yorkshire attack – when compared to the Gloucester fireball, David Lawrence.

As England and Australia gathered at Trent Bridge yesterday for the third Test, there was a sense that the Ashes series, which has so far seemed just a little like shadow boxing, might be about to take a critical turn. England could afford to lose at Lord's; it may even have helped the English game by bumping up the takings here. A second defeat, leaving England to win two of the last three tests to have a hope of regaining the Ashes, would be potentially disastrous.

Yet it seems probable that someone will win. Of the last 15 Tests in this country, 14 have produced a result, and there has not been a draw on this ground since 1976.

It was overcast and muggy yesterday, but there was no hint of rain. And the pitch looked as if it might just be a beauty. At Nottingham that no longer necessarily means one on which teams can bat to perdition, but one with a little something for everyone: a bit of life on the first day, runs on the second and third, turn by Monday and bounce all round.

These two teams do not look very draw-minded. Peter May has told his players to curb some of their exuberance and try to build big hundreds. 'The theme is patience, in batting and bowling,' he said yesterday. But the nature of Gooch (who is due for a score), Gower, Botham and even Robinson, is that if they stay at the crease the runs will come quickly enough. That is not a bad thing. The trick is staying there.

Australia may further equip themselves for a positive result by dropping a batsman – the out-of-form Wood is the obvious favourite, which would mean Wessels reverting to opener – and including an extra quick bowler, which would be the uncapped Dave Gilbert rather than Thomson.

That would give the Australians a pretty formidable fast attack, and one which England can hardly hope to match. More than once in recent years the selectors are thought to have argued in favour of including two spinners with successive captains who were anxious to surround themselves with as many seamers as possible. That pattern may continue this morning, although the presence of Gooch, who could be very useful if the air hints at swing as much as it did yesterday, adds an extra option, which strengthens the case for playing Botham, Edmonds and Emburey and leaving out, one presumes, Sidebottom.

The pressure is on England, though with the captaincy secure for the summer, it is now slightly off Gower personally. An Ealing reader has responded to my criticism of Gower over the double-nightwatchman incident which, I suggested, showed he lacked the extra mystical dimension of captaincy, by saying this was 'a little like condemning Moses for not being able to walk on water and resorting instead to the rather prosaic expedient of dividing the seas.'

This is a sharp answer, but I believe the best captains would have sensed the psychological importance of emerging themselves on the Saturday night at Lord's, which Gower did not. I do think Gower, with his gifts of chairmanship, could be a most effective captain of an effective team. Let us say it again: England may be just one strike bowler away from becoming that. For their immediate prospects we must hope that bowler is either Agnew or Sidebottom.

FIRST DAY

Nottingham, Friday 12 July

England yesterday recaptured the initiative from Australia and, who knows, may have laid the foundations for the recapture of the Ashes with a display of spectacular batting domination in the third Test at Trent Bridge. They finished the opening day (shortened by 10 overs through bad, if not dangerous light) on 279 for two, David Gower leading the way with an unbeaten century; the Australians finished entirely demoralised.

It rather serves them right. Having toyed with the idea of including the extra pace bowler Dave Gilbert, they instead stuck to the conservative policy of a four-man attack. This may be fair enough for a team with four entirely trustworthy bowlers, but these Australians are a good deal iffier than that. The tone for the day was set by McDermott presenting Gooch with about a month's ration of full tosses, which gave England the edge from the start. And the Australian ground fielding was, at times, almost as ragged as the bowling.

The Australians were suffering anyway. They have had an outbreak of gastroenteritis, as if this were a tour of Pakistan. Hilditch, who is playing, and Matthews, on the fringe, were the worst sufferers yesterday but Holland was starting to show symptoms in the evening and Lawson was worrying about cramp.

But the positive side of the play was that, as at Madras and Leeds, England's most promising batting team for a generation began to add achievement to talent. Gower's 107 not out was his third century off the Australians this summer but his first for 14 Tests; Gooch's 70, which came after some premature warning

shots across his bow from the morning tabloids, was his first home
Test 50 against Australia in 21 attempts; Gatting, 53 not out, is
closing on his highest against Australia.

The nearest thing to a failure was Robinson, the supposed
steadying influence, who raced to 38 in barely an hour when the
bowling was at its most tempting, then got out. There has not
been England batting like it in an Ashes Test at Nottingham since
the match of Paynter's double century in 1938.

Patience, according to Peter May, was going to be the theme.
That, one supposes, meant waiting for the bad ball. It just happens
that the batsmen rarely had to wait long.

It was, above all, Gower's day. He began by ending his sequence
of six losing tosses in Tests (using a 10 franc coin to confuse
Border) and chose to bat on a pitch that turned out to be more
like Nottingham Ancient than Modern. The soft underbelly beneath the firm top meant there was no pace, a product presumably
of both the wet June and the groundsman Ron Allsopp's determination to avoid a repeat of the embarrassing 1981 pitch. England read it as slow and left out Agnew, giving Sidebottom, who
has had an extraordinary couple of weeks, his Test debut after all.

Yet conditions might have helped a more resilient attack. It was
grey and blowy, and our homeliest Test ground was at something
less than its best or fullest. But there was a determination about
the England batsmen. One theory is that they were annoyed by
the pen pictures of them in the *Daily Express* by Phil Edmonds's
wife Frances, who has a whiplash turn of phrase in several lan-
guages. Actually, her most perceptive paragraph was the description of her husband as a closet Establishment man. To love him
is to know him, no doubt.

Even Robinson ('one of nature's gentlemen' – Frances Edmonds) could not stop scoring until he tried to drive a Lawson
delivery that straightened. Gooch was much more sombre: he took
25 minutes to score a run and although 48 came in the first nine
overs, he made only 12 of them. But McDermott was generous –
until he overdid the full tosses and toppled Gooch with a beamer
– and Lawson non-penetrative; and Gooch's class came through.

Gower started by missing his first ball and only just got away
from the second. But thereafter he played quality strokes with less
hint of risk than at Lord's. On a radio chat show on Wednesday

night he had sounded his former assured self once more, the young man of the world. And this rediscovered confidence showed on the field. When Holland tried to buy his wicket, Gower made it clear that he was going to drive a very hard bargain indeed. His tenth Test hundred took three and threequarter hours. He is back on his pedestal, and a good thing too.

Before tea Gooch punched a low catch to gully. Gatting too was a long while on nought. And the applause for his first run – from a crowd who have long resented his appearances ahead of Randall – was a shade ironic. But by the time he reached his 50 after an innings of sense and power, even Nottingham had started to warm to him. Gower last night was talking of scoring 600, the sooner the better. If Gatting can make a big slice of that, years of ill-feeling will melt away.

SECOND DAY

Nottingham, Saturday 13 July

England's assault on a batting Everest ran out of oxygen some-where around the South Col yesterday. Six hundred, said David Gower on Thursday night; 456 all out said the Trent Bridge score board at teatime yesterday. And since the board also read Aus-tralia 94 for one at the close, a day that had glittered with possi-bilities for England ended with the draw starting to look a tedious probability.

After two days of the third Test, England still led by 362. One assumes they are already defeat-proof, although England scored 450-plus and lost at Leeds in 1948 and at Melbourne in 1928–29. There can have been very few teams in history who were ever 358 for two and then lost.

It was an old-fashioned collapse to go with the old-fashioned Nottingham pitch. It seems to me that far too much time in cricket is spent these days watching capable but unexciting later batsmen fiddle about. Tailenders should be either rumbustious or incom-petent, except in situations of extreme crisis, when they are al-lowed to be gallant. There was just a hint of incompetence about the way England contrived to lose their last eight wickets for 98, the middle four of them in 11 deliveries. It was rather startling from a team in which only Sidebottom has not made a Test 50.

But one part of the collapse was quite encouraging for England; Lamb was leg before to a not very full delivery from Lawson that skidded through – the first sign that what one spectator called the 'de-Hadleefied' pitch might be something less than a batsman's friend by the later stages. Lamb, however, may have found it hard to look on the bright side.

So might Gower. For almost two hours it was hard to see where Australia were ever going to find another wicket. The gates were closed; the weather, though the sun shone only occasionally, was nicely bracing, like Skegness on a good day; and the crowd were all set for the ascent – the Gower 200, the Gatting 100, whatever.

The Australians' afflicted stomachs were better yesterday and their bowling improved steadily throughout the innings, but then it started from a very low base, and by this time Gower and Gatting were entrenched. They began the day cautiously – only 23 in the first hour – but saw off the new ball and, as Lawson and

---

Gatting gone: the expressions back up the unlikely story. Holland parried Gower's drive on to the bowler's stumps with Gatting, backing up, out of his ground.

McDermott tired, Gower began to unleash a selection of These Strokes You Have Loved, mainly off the back foot.

Australia needed a fluke, and they got it. Gower straight-drove Holland, who parried the ball on to the stumps with Gatting, on 74, out of his ground. Curiously, the same thing had almost happened to Gower on Thursday. But he did not have much time left at the crease to think about that. O'Donnell found him undecided and Phillips took the catch. Gower's 166 had taken just over six hours.

There was not even much chance for Gower to savour that. Thirty-five minutes after lunch came Lamb's mishap, and Botham lofted to mid-off next ball. He had made 38 in even time with seven fours and, as ever, no one had dared go to the loo or blink while Botham was batting. But somehow one had sensed that it was not going to be one of the great days and it was not, for Botham or anyone else.

Downton was out for his second successive first ball nought, to a super diving catch from Ritchie at square leg. 'Of all people,' said the whole of Australia in unison, since Ritchie is not famous for such things. Sidebottom's first Test innings was also brief, and 416 for four had become 419 for eight. There were a few runs left, but not many. Australia were in after tea, and Lawson had found himself with five wickets in a Test innings for the 10th time without ever firing at full pace.

Australia set off in pursuit after tea, with 257 to avoid the follow-on the first priority. That did not look a problem. Hilditch's hook was in better order than it has been (as was his previously dicky stomach). The England attack, with Botham now the undisputed downwind bowler, looked much steadier than Australia's, but a bit toothless. Perhaps Saturday will again inspire Botham. But it might have been more interesting to see what a really fast bowler would have made of this pitch.

There were a few further signs of uneven bounce towards evening. And, eventually, Allott made the breakthrough, with Hilditch being lbw pushing forward to a ball that would probably have shaved leg stump. By then, Wood, after a run of failures, was starting to look set. After the nightwatchman, Wessels will be in. Englishmen will arrive at the ground this morning with a much more measured tread than they did yesterday.

THIRD DAY

Nottingham, Monday 15 July

Australia start the fourth day of the third Cornhill Test at Trent Bridge today on 366 for five, 90 behind England. It is possible that the Australians could collapse this morning and find themselves in trouble in the fourth innings; it is also possible that they could go on to 600 or so and put England under pressure. But it will take some rough batting somewhere for anything to materialise; the overwhelming probability is stalemate.

In this situation it is not surprising that Saturday was not the most riveting day of the series, despite batting of great determination from Graeme Wood and Greg Ritchie. However, you know how it is with Saturday afternoon, full grounds, and Botham - he has to do something. I think he must have a private arrangement with the Sunday papers. And, in the unfortunate absence of runs and wickets, he got into a row.

Before Botham was seen on television airing his opinions for the benefit of lip-readers, he had been on the wrong end of almost every misfortune a bowler can receive from an umpire. In quick and extraordinary succession, Alan Whitehead had rejected a superb boundary catch by Edmonds on the grounds that it was a no-ball; turned down an exceptionally promising lbw shout; warned Botham informally (as he had done with Lawson) for overdoing the bouncer; and formally (à la McDermott) for trespassing on the pitch; and furthermore refused England's entreaties that the ball was out of shape.

There were words between Whitehead, Botham and Gower. Botham was bowling with his blood up, which is what England require of him, and he addressed the nation in temper and in close-up. The text, I believe, was: 'Oh, dear; oh, botheration; oh, fiddlesticks.' Whitehead, everyone insisted afterwards, had no complaints about the language. Peter May, the chairman of selectors, was apparently driving home at the time and only heard the radio description. He plans to hold an inquiry after the match.

Whitehead has only umpired one Test before, in 1982. He was a Somerset player himself, although the dressing-room then was rather different. He looks a bit like a new maths master who has

Border at Trent Bridge: the loneliness of command, the possibility of defeat.

been warned in the staff room that he must not let the Lower Fifth rag him. The smack of firm umpiring is not an unwelcome sound, and good luck to him. There should have been more of it last summer.

Unfortunately, Whitehead has almost certainly made a mistake by giving Border caught at slip. It did not look as if Border had hit the ball. When asked, he said with Australian directness that he had not, although he softened the denial with kind words about rough and smooth and the high standards of English umpiring generally. I am sure Border was telling the truth, both because he is that sort, and because he currently has runs like a dog has fleas, and has no need to lie. But I think I prefer the Willis–Gower policy of public silence in these matters.

Fortunately for Australia, the runs came from elsewhere, and Wood was still there at the close on 152, having batted $8\frac{1}{2}$ hours for his eighth Test century. It was a most improbable one. Wood has been right out of form, both in Tests (six games without a 50)

Botham's way: this time umpire Alan Whitehead, who spent much of the Trent Bridge Saturday thwarting Botham, allows his appeal for a slip catch against Border. TV replays suggested the ball came off the pad. Edmonds, Downton and the short-leg Hassan back up the appeal. Wood is the other batsman.

and on the tour (77 runs in eight innings). He was desperately close to being dropped to accommodate a fifth bowler. Even at his best, he is regarded as a poor player of decent spin, which is what he faced during most of Saturday from Edmonds and Emburey, on a pitch gradually giving them more help. And he has never been a maker of big Test hundreds: his previous best was 126.

Australia's faith in him was rewarded. Wood showed judgment, composure, skill and stamina; and if for strokeplay and joy he was not in the same league as Gower, the two innings have effectively cancelled each other out.

The day's aesthetic pleasure came from the Queenslander, Ritchie, who has scored 65 of the unbroken stand of 103. Ritchie has always invited comparisons with Peter Burge, whose innings at Leeds won the 1964 series for Australia, both because of the suspicion of flab (Burge, who now looks like Stratford Johns, was known as 'The fastest-growing sport in Queensland') and the handsomeness of his cutting and driving. Ritchie may even become the better player: the growing maturity of his batting and the improvement in his fielding have been major pluses for Australia in this series.

Wood and Ritchie, it must be said, were facing an England attack that looked short of extra zip from the outset, and was eventually without both Allott, who discovered that stomach bugs are not an exclusively Australian affliction, and Sidebottom, who in the midst of his nineteenth steady but hardly threatening over found that his left big toe had split, horribly and bloodily. Allott was thought the more likely to return today, and some people speculated that Sidebottom had bowled his last ball in Test cricket, although predicting the next move in his career seems extremely hazardous at present.

England were in need of both Band-Aid and Live Aid. But already Allott's illness had given rise to the strange case of the double substitute; this week's successor to the double-nightwatchman, but one that reflects far more credit on Gower's nous.

The official twelfth man in place of Agnew was Paul Parker of Sussex, probably the best out-to-mid-fielder in the country, and he came on for Allott. This meant a thirteenth man was required, and Basharat Hassan was discovered around the ground; at 41, he no longer makes the Nottinghamshire first team, and, that very morning, had announced his intention of retiring.

But Hassan is a specialist short-leg, even at his age. And, with the spinners trying to attack, England had need of that. So, after Allott had made a brief but unsuccessful attempt to resume, Hassan emerged with his helmet to protect the nerves and limbs of more important people, while Parker stayed inside until Sidebottom's injury.

Prior to 1980, Australia could have objected to the use of a specialist sub in this manner. However, the law has changed. Gower was asked who thought of the Hassan ploy.

'Why?' he inquired. 'Was it a good one?'

'Yes, rather.'

'Oh well, my idea, then.'

Did Allott come back solely as a way of getting Parker off and Hassan on?

'Don't give me too much credit,' Gower said. 'I'm not that subtle.'

I don't know, though: Gower's lovely batting has already uplifted an otherwise disappointing match. We might just be starting to see hidden depths to his captaincy. If he can direct Botham's fire away from the umpires and back to the batsmen, then we will really be getting somewhere.

FOURTH DAY

Nottingham, Tuesday 16 July

During the gaps in play yesterday, the TV showed extracts from the Old Trafford Tests of 1961 and 1968, both of them among the great England pig's ears of all time.

Trent Bridge 1985 might just rank in the same league if the batsmen were to go out and play like pools winners this morning. But all the signs at the end of the fourth day were that this year's third Test was going to rank with Old Trafford 1964, another

---

Wood on his way to 172, an innings of dedication and commitment.

match remembered with great affection by several batsmen but by almost no one else.

Australia were bowled out shortly after tea yesterday for 539, a first innings lead of 83. England scored eight for nought in their second innings before bad light put paid to the last 18 overs. A surprisingly large crowd, given the situation, gave a surprisingly spirited jeer.

This match seems to mark a pause for stocktaking in an eventful series. Ron Allsopp, the Trent Bridge groundsman who has been blamed so often for preparing bowlers' pitches, has produced one far too bland for the two teams' sub-standard attacks.

Australia's was understrength from the start. By yesterday so was England's, with Sidebottom out of the contest and Allott still a bit groggy. England were probably understrength qualitively as well. When battle resumes at Old Trafford next month, they really must include one bowler of extra pace, no matter how unpromising the pitch. His identity – Cowans, Agnew, Lawrence or Dilley, take your pick – is less important than the principle.

Australia progressed from 366 for five to a first-innings lead, and their highest score against England since Melbourne 1965–66, 54 Ashes Tests ago. And it was the highest score by the worst Australian team ever to come here, at least since the last time some damn fool used that phrase, which was probably on the last tour. The highlight was Greg Ritchie's maiden Ashes century, 146. Wood was out for 172, the victim of the only bit of theatre all day which matched the norm for the series.

Naturally, it involved Botham. He had been kept out of the attack for 90 minutes, perhaps on Brearley's principle that he has to get angry before he can bowl at his best (on reflection, most of Botham's great wicket-taking performances have come late in the day). This time Gower kept him away from umpire Whitehead and before Botham started from the Pavilion End, umpire Constant playfully slapped his hand to tell him not to be naughty.

He did not need to be. The first ball was short, and Wood pulled it to mid-wicket, where Robinson fielded. The second was also short: similar shot, similar placement, only this time Robinson took it on the full – Test victim No. 327 for Botham. Thank you very much. Wood, though, had batted 10 hours since Friday teatime, an innings of utter dedication.

Ritchie's batting was a different matter. When he reached his 100, after several more delicious blows, mainly on the on-side, he raised his bat like a world champion. Thereafter he kept his toothy grin throughout. There is a boyish delight to Ritchie's batting but, increasingly, a man's judgment.

Ritchie survived the departure of Phillips, who did an undignified over-balancing act while Emburey drifted a ball on to the left-hander's leg stump. Then Ritchie marched out of his crease to drive Edmonds and, after six hours, was beaten by both flight and turn. Most of the time the spinners could only press on dutifully and hope for something out of the rough. Edmonds might have had O'Donnell caught bat-and-pad by England's temporary specialist stuntman Hassan. But, alas, dear old Bash missed the chance, which may cut the incipient demand for freelance have-helmet-will-travel short-legs.

O'Donnell found his way to 46 before Botham whipped out both him and Lawson in successive balls, which puts him on a hat-trick when Australia start their second innings. If they ever do. The light, once again, was pretty marginal when the batsmen were allowed to come off, but a grey, permanent-looking drizzle followed on behind. If a day has to be lost to rain this summer, today would be a very reasonable candidate.

FIFTH DAY

Nottingham, Wednesday 17 July

The third Cornhill Test finally ended in a draw at 5.30 last night. Long since, it had turned into The Wasteland Test: breeding improved batting averages out of the dead game, mixing memory and desire to get home.

The last day was shortened by $1\frac{3}{4}$ hours: overnight rain delayed the start, and no one wanted the optional half-hour at the close. Even so, one felt at the finish rather as one does at the end of a very long plane journey with a rotten film.

England, technically needing 83 to avoid an innings defeat, moved their second innings from eight for no wicket to 196 for two, with Robinson batting throughout the $4\frac{1}{2}$-hour innings to score 77 not out – his fifth 50 in his first eight Tests. His Test average now is 64, way ahead of Viv Richards and the likes of Hobbs and Hutton. He can hardly keep that up, but already Robinson has made one of the great international starts of all time. Even Bradman got dropped after his first Test.

These runs were fairly meaningless, although someone had to stay out there to avoid the outside chance of defeat. Some people had imagined that the leg-spinner, Holland, might give England problems as the pitch wore. Both Holland and pitch turned out to be quite innocuous. One ball from O'Donnell kept very low at the end. Batting might have become really uncomfortable by the twelfth day.

After this, no one will mind the little recess ahead of us. There are 15 days instead of the usual eight before the fourth Test starts at Old Trafford, and most of the England players will play two whole successive games for their counties.

Everyone agrees that England and Australia are well matched. But the feeling at half-time must be that Australia are narrowly ahead on points. Since they hold the Ashes, three more draws would suit them fine.

The Australian players should also all get a couple of first-class games before Old Trafford. Wellham will be pressing for Boon's place, although the four-bowler policy is by no means certain to continue: Manchester could well be the place to bring in the slow left-armer, Bennett.

England's concern, as ever, will be seam bowling. The selectors are thought to have earmarked the Gloucestershire-Glamorgan match on Saturday week (a year ago, the last place in the world anyone would have looked for fast bowlers) as the occasion to compare David Lawrence with Greg Thomas. But the next team will be chosen before that starts, and if Lawrence can produce one more devastating burst in the meantime he will become hard to ignore.

The present attack were able to keep out of sight yesterday while Australia struggled. Two wickets fell: Gooch and Robinson

---

Bob Holland, the man who might just have bowled Australia to an improbable victory. But this was not the pitch, and Holland, whose bowling turned out to be disappointingly unvaried, not a dangerous enough leg-spinner.

England v. Australia

at Trent Bridge

11, 12, 13, 15, 16 July 1985

E N G L A N D

		1st Innings				2nd Innings		
1	G A GOOCH	ct Wessels	b Lawson	70		ct Ritchie	b McDermott	48
2	R T ROBINSON	ct Border	b Lawson	38		not out		77
3	*D I GOWER	ct Phillips	b O'Donnell	166		ct Phillips	b McDermott	17
4	M W GATTING	run out		74		not out		35
5	A J LAMB	lbw	b Lawson	17				
6	I T BOTHAM	ct O'Donnell	b McDermott	38				
7	+P R DOWNTON	ct Ritchie	b McDermott	0				
8	J E EMBUREY	not out		16				
9	P H EDMONDS		b Holland	12				
10	P J W ALLOTT	ct Border	b Lawson	7				
11	A SIDEBOTTOM	ct O'Donnell	b Lawson	2				

Extras 16
TOTAL 456

Extras 19
TOTAL 196 - 2

Wkts	1	2	3	4	5	6	7	8	9		1	2	3	4	5	6	7	8	9
Fell	55	171	358	365	416	416	419	419	443		79	107							

Bowling Analysis	O	M	R	WK	W	NB		O	M	R	WK	W	NB
LAWSON GF	39.4	10	103	5	1	2+1		13	4	32	–	–	1
McDERMOTT CJ	35	3	147	2	–	1		16	2	42	2	–	1+1
O'DONNELL SP	29	4	104	1	–	–		10	2	26	–	–	–
HOLLAND RG	26	3	90	1	–	–		28	9	69	–	–	–
RITCHIE GM				1 run out				1	–	10	–	–	–

A U S T R A L I A

		1st Innings				2nd Innings
1	A M J HILDITCH	lbw	b Allott	47		
2	G M WOOD	ct Robinson	b Botham	172		
3	K C WESSELS	ct Downton	b Emburey	33		
4	*A R BORDER	ct Botham	b Edmonds	23		
5	G M RITCHIE		b Edmonds	146		
6	D C BOON	ct & bld	Emburey	15		
7	+W B PHILLIPS		b Emburey	2		
8	S P O'DONNELL	ct Downton	b Botham	46		
9	G F LAWSON	ct Gooch	b Botham	18		
10	C J McDERMOTT	not out		0		
11	R G HOLLAND	lbw	b Sidebottom	10		

Extras 27
TOTAL 539

Extras
TOTAL

Wkts	1	2	3	4	5	6	7	8	9		1	2	3	4	5	6	7	8	9
Fell	87	128	205	234	263	424	437	491	539										

Bowling Analysis	O	M	R	WK	W	NB		O	M	R	WK	W	NB
BOTHAM IT	34.2	3	107	3	2	3							
SIDEBOTTOM A	18.4	3	65	1	–	9							
ALLOTT PJW	18	4	55	1	–	–							
EDMONDS PH	66	18	155	2	–	–							
EMBUREY JE	55	15	129	3	–	–							
GOOCH GA	8.2	2	13	–	–	–							
GATTING MW	1	–	2	–	–	–							

ENGLAND WON THE TOSS AND ELECTED TO BAT

* Captain
+ Wicket-keeper

Umpires: DJ CONSTANT
AGT WHITEHEAD

Scorers: L BEAUMONT
M RINGHAM

Man of the Match adjudicator:
Mr T W GRAVENEY

M A T C H   D R A W N   MAN OF THE MATCH - DAVID GOWER had their best opening stand so far, 79, before Gooch mis-pulled to mid-wicket; then Gower, who pulled one smashing four off Holland, had one of his firm-footed wafts and was caught behind. Gower was still named Man of the Match by Tom Graveney, ahead of Wood and Ritchie. Some Australians greeted this news with disbelief, but then his 166 does seem an awfully long time ago.

There was one uncomfortable moment for Robinson when McDermott again produced a near-beamer, to which he is prone, and Robinson got a finger jammed, to which he is prone. But he batted on after treatment from Nottinghamshire's lady physio, and there was no ill-feeling.

The only trace of that came later when Border gave his views on some of the Sunday papers, which barely mentioned Wood's century amidst stuff about Botham, not all of that wholly accurate. 'Pretty ordinary reporting,' Border thought.

But even that was said calmly and placidly. And it is true that Wood's innings will stand in Wisden forever. Botham's little ruckus with umpire Whitehead is likely to be forgotten very quickly; it seems highly improbable that the TCCB will take any action.

Most placid of all, apart from the pitch, were the spectators. Those who were daffy enough to want to pay to see yesterday's play were kept waiting outside until the umpires announced play could start; Nottinghamshire said they did not want to take their money for nothing. I think they should all have been paid, at least at the Equity extras' rate.

FOURTH TEST — OLD TRAFFORD

Monday 29 July

The winner of this weekend's star prize is Richard Ellison, the 25-year-old Kent all-rounder, who has been named in the 12 for the fourth Test at Old Trafford on Thursday in place of Arnie Sidebottom, who made a brief and not especially happy entry into Test cricket at Trent Bridge.

The pattern of the past two Tests has been that the centre of attention on Sunday has been quite forgotten by two minutes past 11 on Thursday morning: Sidebottom discovered this at Lord's and Jonathan Agnew at Trent Bridge. Now Ellison must be the favourite to be 12th man, and it may be that the quiet retention of Agnew will be more relevant to the outcome of the match.

In the end, after a fortnight of mostly circular argument about England's fast bowling resources, the selectors did not have a vast amount of choice. Sidebottom is injured, as are Foster, John Lever, Greg Thomas and Gladstone Small. Sidebottom's 18 completed overs on the unresponsive Nottingham turf hardly constituted a fair trial, but it has been hard all along to find anyone outside the selection panel who regarded him as any kind of answer.

There was the Syd Lawrence bandwagon; but that stopped rolling last Thursday, when Alec Bedser arrived at Bristol to see this summer's sensation and watched him have one of his worst days. It is accepted now that Lawrence has a lot to learn; this must include the art of picking off-days more cleverly.

That left Cowans as Ellison's only serious rival, though it is thought that Dilley and Les Taylor got honourable mentions. But unless conditions look particularly suited to Ellison's outswing, it is most probable that Agnew, Allott and Botham will divide the

The twins: When the re-runs of the 1981 Old Trafford Test were shown, Paul Allott (left) was a bespectacled studious-looking young man; Ian Botham was short-haired and comparatively clean-cut too. By 1985 they had developed new images – but at the cost of some individuality.

new ball between them, as in the final two Tests of last summer, backed up by the two spinners Edmonds and Emburey.

Ellison's recall is a reward for current form. After trouble with an early season injury, he has taken 42 wickets and played a major role in Kent's leap up the table. He first entered the national consciousness exactly a year ago when he was in the 12 for the Old Trafford Test against the West Indies. He was lucky enough to be 12th man for that disaster, and played in the next five, keeping Foster out of the first three in India.

Ellison is apparently becoming a more subtle as well as a big swinger of the ball, but it remains hard to see him running through Test batsmen; he is also a very respectable No. 8 bat, though not necessarily against Holland's leg spin.

If the skies are as grey and moody as they were yesterday, then it might well be sensible to include him. One just hopes the selectors do not ignore genuine pace, represented here by Agnew, yet again merely because the pitch looks slow as, at Old Trafford, it probably will be.

The evidence of Cowans's performance in India (and Marshall's last summer and Lawrence's at Gloucester earlier this month) is that a really fast bowler can bowl fast on anything, at least if he pitches the ball up. Cowans's continued omission, on the basis of one bad match at Leeds, remains a little puzzling, and personally irritating. I happen to know that last occasion when five Middlesex players were picked for England and am dying for the chance to mention it. (Oh, very well then. Lord's 1949 against New Zealand: George Mann, the captain, Denis Compton, Bill Edrich, Jack Robertson and Jack Young. England had the worse end of a draw, and only Compton and Edrich survived into the next Test. Freddie Brown took over the captaincy.)

England's worries apart from the fast bowling are all minor. Robinson is expected to be fit by Thursday; if not, his county colleague Chris Broad would probably come back. The middle order hopefuls are all still kicking at a locked door, though there is just a hint of worry about Lamb's form for England; Bill Athey now appears to have gone ahead of Randall and Chris Smith at the front of the throng, but Lamb is almost certainly in place for at least two more Tests.

The same goes for Downton. The only person everyone can

agree is a better wicketkeeper is 39-year-old Alan Knott, whose batting has declined and would not want to tour, though if David East keeps taking eight catches in an innings, as he did on Saturday, he might be in the frame.

But there is little wrong with England at present that would not be cured by a handsome win in Manchester. Peter May can even console himself that Botham is learning patience. He took a full 92 minutes over his daily century on Saturday, almost twice as long as on Friday. By the time the Test starts, he might really be building an innings.

Manchester, Thursday 1 August

It was dry in Manchester yesterday, but very grey, and the wind smelt of September. Had the Test been under way Dickie Bird would have been reaching for the light meter. The Australians are starting to look at us with a wild and pitying surmise – you mean to say you live in a climate like this?

Even by local standards, Old Trafford has had a lot of rain lately and, assuming the fourth Test can start on time this morning, the pitch is likely to be damp and the outfield sluggish.

Lancashire will be more than normally anxious to ensure the weather does not beat them. Five weeks ago, the Lord's ground staff made prodigious efforts to get their Test started on time after all the downpours. Originally, this game was also going to take place at Lord's and Manchester was going to miss out.

That plan was halted after Cedric Rhoades, the Lancashire chairman, had unleashed wrath from the north of a fury not seen since the last Jacobite Rebellion collapsed. It is important to the club that this Test is a success.

Advance ticket sales have been magnificent (close to £250,000, easily a ground record), so if it stays fine there will be no problem. And no one expects a repetition of Trent Bridge. It is most unlikely that the pitch will have any pace, but conditions yesterday suggested swing, seam and spin at various stages and left both camps even more uncertain than usual about final selection.

England would probably like to play all their 12. Both Robinson and Ellison proved themselves fit, so there are no complica-

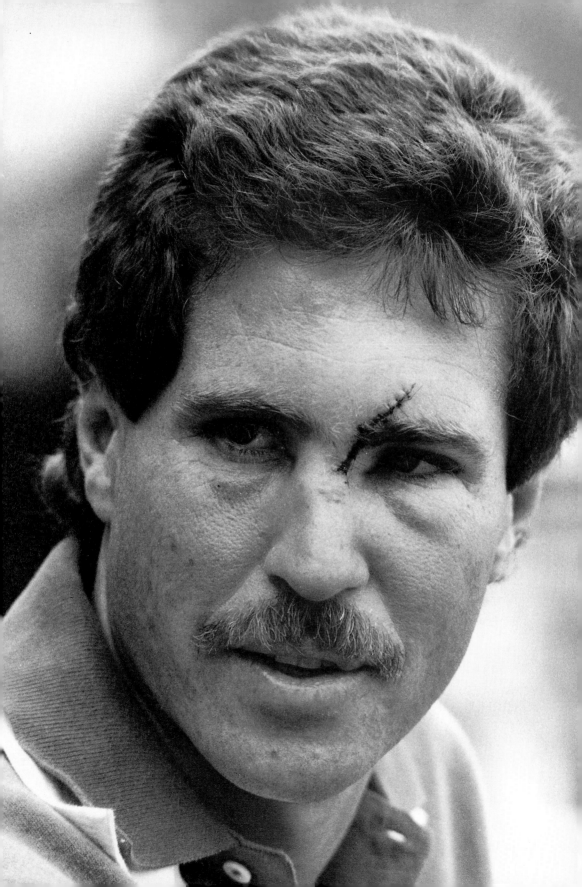

tions there. But England do not want to leave out Agnew in view of his nine for 70 against Kent on Monday, which was also on a slow wicket, but they also want Ellison's swing and the two spinners. It is an open contest and either Edmonds or Emburey may have to go. But, home ground or not, Allott might turn out to be the unlucky one.

The Australians were also deferring their choice and, I think, with less clarity of purpose. The four-bowler obsession may not be dead yet and they have no obvious batsman to drop to accommodate a fifth bowler. Wood, their saviour at Nottingham, is thought to have recovered from his blow on the face at Northampton last Saturday and Boon, a complete failure so far in the Tests, made a double century there.

There has been some speculation that the Australians would drop O'Donnell and play a half-fit Lawson with the inexperienced McDermott, but only play two spinners. I dare say England would be delighted by that: a more sensible possibility would have been the return of Thomson, but he was left out of the 13 announced last night which added Gilbert and Matthews to the Nottingham eleven.

In weather like this, the Australians would prefer to be playing footy or rugby league rather than cricket. And one feels that if this Test can be won, it should be won by England. They are backed by recent history. England have won the last three Manchester Tests against Australia, though they went half a century without a win here before Laker's match in 1956. But as one hunts for historical analogies, one gets an increasing feeling that this series more than anything resembles the triangular tournament of 1912: England v. Australia v. South Africa.

The South Africans gained another recruit yesterday when Michael Haysman, the 24-year-old South Australian batsman who played for Leicestershire last summer, walked over the dead body of the Australian Cricket Board to join the rebels for the forthcoming tour.

Brave face: Graeme Wood, whose century at Trent Bridge was followed by a blow above the nose while batting at Northampton. He was forced to withdraw from the Old Trafford Test, and in his last four innings of the series made only 57 runs.

(Twenty-four hours earlier, the Australian Cricket Board had settled its court case with the South Africans and banned Kim Hughes and the other players planning to go on two rebel tours: from Test cricket for three years and from domestic cricket for two years. Since the rebels had effectively banned themselves for two years by signing for the two tours, this must constitute one of the most meaningless punishments in history.)

Meanwhile, Graham Gooch, Essex's answer to Edith Piaf, has tried to clarify the 'no regrets' comment that has annoyed Caribbean governments and cast a lingering shadow over England's winter tour. Gooch said yesterday that he had not meant to imply that he was about to disappear to South Africa again. 'In the circumstances prevailing in 1982 I would go again. I have no regrets about what I did, but that's nothing new. It's not to say that if I was offered a trip now, I would go now.'

FIRST DAY

Manchester, Friday 2 August

In the music hall, the first turn after the interval was always a novelty act: jugglers or acrobats or something. The Test series resumed at Old Trafford yesterday, after its brief interval, with a decided novelty: the England spinners took the first four wickets.

There was then something rather more familiar, a late burst of wicket-taking by Botham. And though there was a nifty last-wicket stand dominated by O'Donnell, the overall effect was still pleasing and a bit of a novelty for England: Australia, put into bat by Gower, 257 all out.

At the Oval last year, England bowled the West Indies out for 190, and a fat lot of good that did. This pitch was as damp and slothful as everyone feared, and it may never turn into a decent one (if the wickets go on getting slower and slower, before long the ball will just stop dead on pitching, like a deck quoit). But it must surely quicken up a bit, and if England's batsmen can apply themselves, they can take a giant stride today towards the Ashes.

The only other time Gower chose to field first as a Test captain was the Sri Lanka game last summer, which is not a happy memory. And when Australia were 71 for none just before lunch and the ground was as quiet as it is during Lancashire's championship matches, uncomfortable thoughts must have been running through the helmsman's mind.

But England turned the day round, partly through bad Australian batting, including a rush of blood from Border, partly through intelligent use of the moisture by the spinners and partly through Botham's use of the supernatural. He finished with four for 79 and Edmonds with four for 40.

It was a cool day, better for a brisk walk on the fells than cricket. The Australians do not relish these conditions. But the ground was close to full, although it stayed eerily quiet compared to the can-clanging West Indian Test last summer, even after England began taking wickets, and there was no trouble with rain or bad light. All day, the clouds over Kinder gradually grew lighter, fluffier and more optimistic.

England left out Ellison which was probably the best of a difficult set of options, and Australia finally decided to play a fifth bowler, the off-spinning all-rounder Matthews, though the decision was partly forced on them by Woods's late withdrawal due to lingering after-effects of his blow in the face at Northampton.

Botham's run-up had to be filled with sawdust to get play started, and one Fleet Street habitué thought it looked like the floor of the Cheshire Cheese. It did not help Botham much. His opening spell was despatched at a rate of five an over with as near as Hilditch and Wessels will ever get to vigour. Agnew made no impact either and England could get no grip on the match at all until Allott appeared to do his steadying job from the Stretford End, and Emburey, after a mere hour, was handed the ball to partner him.

Suddenly, Wessels drove to slip (Botham had to be involved one way or another), the first time a spinner has taken England's opening wicket in a home Test for seven years or more. And after lunch Edmonds became involved: Hilditch was caught at silly point off his arm ball; Border, whose form may have given him delusions of immortality, danced down the track and was stumped; three balls later Ritchie, committed on the back foot, was beaten by a bit of fizz and was caught and bowled.

In one over, England had got rid of the two biggest threats and the Cheshire Cheese was covered by fielders looking like Cheshire

The end of Border, and of a strange sequence: Downton gets a stumping, the first by any England wicket-keeper in a home Test for five years.

cats. (It happens that all three England seam bowlers were Cheshire-born so this is not entirely whimsical.) The stumping, not especially difficult but competent enough, was England's first at home since Bairstow dismissed Wood (for 112) in the centenary Test five years ago.

A stand of 71, equalling the opening one, came next between the low-slung Boon whose build and strength were suited by the pitch and the wicket-keeper, Phillips. There was only one thing for Gower to do. Straight after tea, he called over Botham and, in that mysterious mood that overtakes our hero/villain (delete to taste) late in the day after he has had time to get riled, he blitzed Australia: four wickets in 45 balls.

There was something of a plan. Botham bowled to the square-cutter Phillips with only two on-side fielders and sure enough

Phillips tried the cut, though this surface being what it is, he could only bottom edge to Downton.

Then Boon was superbly caught for 61, off a full-blooded lash, by Lamb at gully. Matthews just shouldered arms, imagining lift and movement that were never there, and his off stump went flying. Lawson was caught behind, and Emburey nipped back to get McDermott, also without offering a shot, first ball.

Botham strikes – again. Australia's second substantial first-day stand, between Boon and Phillips, ends with Phillips attempting a cut and getting a bottom-edge to Downton.

Australia were now 224 for nine, but here Gower overdid the trust in his prince. Botham looking tired, allowed O'Donnell to shield Holland, and put together the third largest stand of the innings.

The spinners should have come back; instead the new ball was taken, but the batsmen did not budge until Edmonds re-appeared and bowled O'Donnell with the last ball of the day.

SECOND DAY

Manchester, Saturday 3 August

So far in this Ashes series there has been a pattern of strangely unsatisfying Fridays all followed by Bothamesque Saturdays. And the cricket at Old Trafford yesterday, dragged down by the pitch, never quite hit the heights.

Yet it went very much according to plan for England, and they finished the second day of the fourth Cornhill Test on 233 for three, only 24 behind Australia and apparently on course for a handsome lead. Botham is next in; everything is set up for him to repeat his 1981 Saturday innings here, perhaps the best he has ever played. Having said that, the beggar will probably get out first ball.

England may have enough in hand already to cope with that. There was a stand of 121 between Gooch and Gower for the second wicket, and Lamb and Gatting saw out the day with a very solid looking partnership. There was luck as well as judgment in England's success. Gooch and Gower had more than their share of false strokes and both were dropped by Boon at first slip – Gower on four, which was vital, and Gooch on 59. This follows pre-match comment about how much better than England's Australia's slip fielding had been.

But the Australians were never quite with it yesterday. McDermott, who took all three wickets, and Lawson produced their best new ball spell of the series but there was no follow up. On a long tour, there is often a point with about a month to go when teams start getting weary. Most of these Australians come from Sydney and Brisbane and on a draughty day in Manchester, immediately after a batting botch-up, it was understandable that they were not

Injury time: umpire Bird, ever in the action, was too close to it when Gooch was batting.

at their best. They may have to raise their spirits as well as their game to save this Test.

With the gates closed yet again and 20,000 people inside Old Trafford, it was a great relief that once more this wretched summer had some mercy on us. There was a morning shower and 40 minutes were lost, but after that it stayed dry and a set of splendid cloudscapes over the Pennines produced nothing untoward. But it felt like autumn, even before 'United's Skipper's Injury Scare' appeared on the *Manchester Evening News* placards.

People thought at the start yesterday that England would be fine if they could grind it out. But the era of Boycott and Tavare is over: 21 came off the first three overs and Robinson was having a bit of a fence when he was caught at second slip in the fourth.

The Gooch/Gower stand was an odd one. They never quite dominated the bowling though there was some fine strokeplay from them both. Gooch drove so straight that he hit the bowler's stumps several times and on one painful occasion umpire Bird's ankle, while Gower, after scoring only 19 between lunch and 10 minutes before tea, then unleashed two stupendous cover drives against O'Donnell.

On 34, midway through his quiet patch, Gower became the ninth Englishman to score 5,000 Test runs. His average, it must be said, is the lowest of the group at 43.21, comparable with Cowdrey and John Edrich, but way behind (in order) Barrington, Hammond, Hutton, Hobbs, Compton and Boycott. But Gower has never bothered about such things; it is part of his charm.

The partnership stayed intact until just after tea, when McDermott came back. The pitch had dried somewhat but was still dead. If this ever becomes the norm it will at least put a stop to the bouncer as a serious weapon. As expected, there were far fewer signs of turn than on Thursday, though one would also expect a leg spinner to extract something where a finger spinner would not. Abdul Qadir or Sivarama would, I think, have spun the ball more than Holland did, though he bowled very tidily. It is Border's business; but it seems very odd that he should show such little urge to use Holland as an attacking bowler with an attacking field.

Since O'Donnell looks even less of a Test wicket-taker, McDermott, who was again in trouble for running on the wicket, had to return to make things happen. Gooch, on 74, was probably just starting to have thoughts of his first and long-awaited Ashes century, when McDermott swung one in and trapped him lbw. In his next over Gower, on 47, played one of his pivoted pick-ups, but only found the long-leg Hilditch, who took a high catch and did extremely well to keep control without falling over the rope.

Gatting and Lamb stayed till the finish. One felt Lamb was going to make a century as he walked out. He is the only man in history to play for England in every match for which he was eligible. Added to that he has developed a wonderful knack of providing the right innings just when people are starting to mutter that it is time to break the sequence. Gatting, despite some strange shots near the close, looked far more in form than might be expected from a man who has reached August without a century.

Through this, Botham was on the balcony, padded up with his headphones on. I doubt if he was listening to Test Match Special, though there was never a serious danger that he would be stopped in whatever tracks he was in. The poor man is said to be suffering from piles, which is not a laughing matter. Piles of runs today and England will be on their way.

THIRD DAY

Manchester, Monday 5 August

I suppose it was all the press's fault, as usual. So many expectations had built up about Jack the Lad's impending innings that it is necessary to divide Saturday's cricket at Old Trafford into three phases, as history masters do with wars: events leading up to Botham, Botham, and post-Botham.

The trouble with this approach is that you get diverted by the clang of battle and miss the changes beneath the surface. Botham on Saturday provided only a brief diversion. Gatting, meanwhile, was providing a further addition to what may well be the real cricketing event of 1985: The Renaissance of English Batsmanship. This morning, England are due to resume their first innings of 448 for six, 191 ahead of Australia. They intend to bat for what Gower wants to be 'a short, sharp and effective' burst before declaring. There is no sign yet of the pitch wearing (if such a turgid muck-heap can ever be described as wearing, or indeed as a pitch), and Australia might be able to bat out five-and-a-bit sessions for the draw. But the evidence so far is that this stinking summer is far more of a threat to England than the opposition; that only a third of Saturday was lost and so little of the 17 previous days of the series is a miracle to make the Rocking Madonna of County Cork look commonplace.

England may or may not win the Fourth Test, but their superiority has been so marked that it is now hard to imagine how Australia could possibly win the series, or save it if the pitches and weather ever improve.

The fifth bowler has made Australia no more effective: Matthews, like O'Donnell, does not look like getting good batsmen out; Holland has lost confidence and the bag containing his googly must have been lost by the airline on the journey out; Lawson is being battered by fate like Graeme Fowler, and has had an asthma attack to contend with on top of a ricked neck. That has left McDermott as the only serious threat. Upwind or downwind, he has bowled like a Trojan, especially when you consider his follow-through problems; but it is an intolerable burden for a 20-year-old.

Still, England look capable of dealing with better attacks. We should have been raving about the stand of 155 between Gatting and Lamb, but Botham's position is now such that it never seemed to be anything more than a prelude. Perhaps only Bradman bestrode a Test in quite this way. Once, the cameras wandered up to the balcony and found him reading a magazine: Marxism Today, I think, or the Times Lit. Supp.

It needed a dead-eye throw from Matthews to get Botham into the action at all. Lamb was out for 67 after six Test innings without a fifty. He was under a bit of pressure, partly because someone has to be, just to make life bearable for county batsmen. He did not make his century but, as ever, he made his point.

In retrospect, it was obvious that Botham would fail: the pitch was too slow, the build-up too great; and he looked as if he wanted to prove the press wrong yet again. Even one of his fours was a patent mishit. He made 20. The hooked ending seemed inevitable.

That left Gatting to breeze on. His highest score, 258 at Bath last summer, was made on another ankle-tapper wicket, and he can adapt to it by playing low and square. In nine Tests since being made vice-captain for India, he has scored 998 runs, almost as many as in the previous 30.

This time he made 160. Gatting himself ranked it behind the

Exit Botham: the innings everyone had been waiting for ends with a shot to deep
backward square, safely held by O'Donnell.

Gatting hooks as a despairing Border waits hopelessly in the slips. Gatting's first home Test century carried England to a lead of 225.

emotional 137 in Bombay and the monumental 207 in Madras, but he needed to do something in England, for everyone to see and believe. Like Bobby Simpson, another slow starter in international cricket, he is now becoming very hard to stop.

With the last of Gatting's inhibitions about batting in Tests peeled away, it really does seem as though England might have a batting line-up to serve them for years to come. The oldest of the big six, Gooch, is only 31. There is no obvious weak link. Of course, patting the ball about at Old Trafford is infinitely different to facing Marshall at Sabina Park – but the basis is there.

If this English revival flowers only briefly, it will almost certainly be because the authorities will have bored the players towards retirement or South Africa by overloading the fixture list. I hope the working party still holding meandering meetings at Lord's to sort out last year's problem – Why England Keep Losing – think long and hard about that.

FOURTH DAY

Manchester, Tuesday 6 August

England start the final day of the fourth Test still pushing for victory, but last night the tide appeared to be ebbing after three hours of fruitless pounding against the world's more impregnable Border outside the Berlin wall. Australia, at the close of the fourth day, were 192 for four in their second innings, 33 runs short of making England bat again. And somehow England have to get rid of the Australian captain.

Four years ago, Border took 377 minutes to score a century here, the slowest-ever by an Australian in Tests, despite a broken finger. He could not quite save that game, but had every intention of doing a bit better this time. After three hours, Border has only 49, including 34 singles, and is bracing himself to bat another six today.

The pitch is showing some signs of age and the England spinners took advantage of the receding hairline to get the four wickets that fell. Emburey, who has recaptured some of his old inventiveness, took three for 56. But the surface is so sluggish that a batsman with a high boredom threshold has a chance of holding out. And once Australia go in front every run will be worth double.

For the first time in the match, the over-achievers yesterday were not England players. The ground staff must have worked amazingly: play started on time, despite Sunday's downpours and their tatty-looking tarpaulins. Whoever controlled the weather was

Flying stumps: McDermott gets his seventh and eighth wickets of England's innings in spectacular fashion – first Edmonds's leg stump goes (*above*), then Allott's middle (*opposite*).

selectively generous again; not a moment was lost, although there was multi-coloured Manchester cloud and much erudite discussion about whether the distant blackness meant Didsbury or Hazel Grove was getting it in the neck.

And above all, there was Craig McDermott; in the first half-hour, Australia's 20-year-old tiger took three more wickets in 14 balls to finish with eight for 141. It was an epic individual performance. In a century of Ashes combat, eight in an innings has only been done 20 times, and never by anyone younger (only Alf Valentine and Venkat had managed this feat younger in any Test). The way McDermott bowled yesterday suggested pace and movement that no one else had extracted all match.

In a sense, only Jim Laker has ever done better. McDermott took all the wickets he could have done: he was prevented from dismissing the other two by Matthews's direct hit on Lamb's stumps on Saturday and Gower's declaration at 482 for nine yesterday morning. His success was partly a reflection on his colleagues' inadequacies, but no-one who saw this can doubt McDermott's potential to become one of the greats.

Australia, none the less, had a huge deficit, 225, and a long haul when they began batting again at midday. They sprang a tactical surprise by opening with Matthews and protecting Wessels from the new ball. England did not use that very well, the pitch combining with Botham's wonky pre-lunch bio-rhythms. But when the spinners came on it was different: the second ball of the afternoon session was driven hard back to Edmonds by Matthews, and when Hilditch played for non-existent turn against Emburey, England were smiling again.

At least they were until they realised that Wessels and Border were now together. Somehow, England had to open this gate, and they settled down for a session of trying to pick the lock with the spinners rather than bashing the door down with Agnew or Botham.

Wessels is an enigma. All season, England have expected him to hit them with one of his tireless innings, just as his boxing opponents might wait for a left hook. But it has not landed. Perhaps Wessels is getting tired of being himself: he might have been caught by Gower at silly point on 10; and he actually played a few of the day's more pleasant strokes until he front-edged a catch back to Emburey immediately before tea. Ten overs later Boon came down the wicket to Emburey, missed, and Australia were 138 for four.

Border could hardly be very angry with Boon – he did much the same himself in the first innings. But there could be no more expansive gestures. That was hard on the naturally attacking Ritchie, all teeth and talent: but apart from one six over the top against Edmonds, he did his part of the defensive job as sturdily as his captain.

If either side went wrong after tea, it was England. Apart from an over from Gatting to let the bowlers change ends – giving Emburey the gale at his back – the two slow bowlers were on unchanged from 2.40 to the close. A blast of Botham might have been an idea as they tired. But the breakthrough could have come. The batsmen's pad play contained much trust in their own judgment and the umpire's. And in the last over, Botham, conscious perhaps that he was in the background for once, led a vociferous appeal for a close catch against Ritchie.

But the new ball is due, and if the breakthrough can come quickly this morning, an England victory should be in its wake – with the Ashes to follow.

Emburey bowling: the first wicket of the match and the last four, but not enough for England.

FIFTH DAY

Manchester, Wednesday 7 August

It was, I suppose, pretty naive to sit in Manchester and believe a favourable weather forecast, but this Test series had been so charmed that anything seemed possible, even a sunny day.

It did not happen. The rain, which had teased England by keeping its distance for most of the first four days, settled on Old Trafford an hour before the start of the fifth and abated only to allow $2\frac{1}{2}$ hours cricket. Australia handled that comfortably, losing only one wicket and saving the fourth Test.

Border, as everyone suspected he would, scored a century – 146 not out. He lost the match award to his pet panther McDermott,

The unstoppable Border: on his way to 146 not out and safety for Australia, this time.

which did not bother him in the least. Australia go to Edgbaston a week tomorrow for the fifth Test still level at 1–1, and with a sudden liking for the climate. Well they do call Australia 'The Lucky Country.'

Overall, almost a whole day was lost. Otherwise, England would surely have won, and Gower preferred to think of it as a moral victory rather than a lost opportunity. But once again the heat, if such a commodity exists in Britain this summer, is on England.

There are only two Tests left now: Edgbaston, with its reputation for belting batsmen's wickets, followed by The Oval, which, it is rumoured, could be the same this year. Amazingly, the last seven Edgbaston Tests, dating back to 1974, have all produced a result inside four days; but the trouble with sequences like that is that they go away as soon as you mention them. If cricket history was among Gower's wide range of interests, he might now be thinking of the summer of 1968, when England were palpably better than Australia but could not get near the Ashes.

Between showers, the players came out four times. One session was curtailed even before the rain, when Gower replaced Edmonds with Allott, which was even less bright than the light. Another did not produce a single ball because the rain came back. At that point Gower chased Border playfully towards the pavilion: I suspect the phrase 'jammy something-or-other' was not far from his lips. And during the dead last hour Botham flummoxed umpire Bird for a moment by filching a bail.

The series is being played in a better spirit than was evident in the sledging Seventies, though I expect someone on Test Match Special tut-tutted. Did Hammond ever play tag with Bradman? But cricket in the Eighties has become too relentless for the participants not to have the odd Christmas Day game of soccer in no-man's-land.

Nonetheless the basics have to come first, and in the day's first over Downton put down Border off Botham. It was a hard catch, off the inside edge and Downton may have done well even to react to the change in direction. But you expect an England wicket-keeper to hold a fair percentage of half-chances, and Downton has not been doing so. It was the wrong player to miss, and enough time was lost yesterday to give people time to mull over alternatives. More than half the country's wicketkeepers might plausibly be mentioned when the selectors meet on Friday.

Cloudscape over Old Trafford. A timeless scene of cricket overcoming the Manchester weather: but for the hospitality boxes behind the sightscreens, the advertising boards and the tower blocks (and maybe the absence of slips), Washbrook and Place or Makepeace and Hallows might be batting.

There is deep reluctance to go back to Knott, who will not tour; and one has to wonder whether Bairstow or Humpage (or French or Russell or Richards or Rhodes or East or Parks or ...) could keep better to unfamiliar spinners than Downton, who knows them.

It was Downton's failure to take Border in the tight Nottingham Test of 1981 that cost him his England place the first time. And Border gave no more chances. Once past 50 he felt safe enough to play some shots, moving to his seventh century of the tour and his 14th in Tests. A comparison with Bradman is like invading a shrine, but surely no Australian captain in the meantime, not even Greg Chappell, has swept his side along behind him in quite this way.

The one batsman to go was Ritchie, who played on to Emburey's second delivery after Gower decided to abort Agnew's use

England v. Australia

FOURTH TEST MATCH AT OLD TRAFFORD

Match Drawn

Man of the Match: C. J. McDermott
Judge: R. Illingworth

Thursday 1st, August 1985
Friday, 2nd, August 1985
Saturday, 3rd, August 1985
Monday, 5th, August 1985
Tuesday, 6th, August 1985
11.00 - 6.00 or 90 overs

ENGLAND

		First Innings		Second Innings
1	G. A. GOOCH	lbw McDermott	74	......
2	R. T. ROBINSON	c Border b McDermott	10	...
* 3	D. I. GOWER	c Hilditch b McDermott	47	......
4	M. W. GATTING	c Phillips b McDermott	160	...
5	A. J. LAMB	run out	67	...
6	I. T. BOTHAM	c O'Donnell b McDermott	20	......
† 7	P. R. DOWNTON	b McDermott	23	......
8	J. E. EMBUREY	not out	31	...
9	P. H. EDMONDS	b McDermott	1	...
10	P. J. W. ALLOTT	b McDermott	7	......
11	J. P. AGNEW	not out	2	...
12	I. P. BUTCHER			

Ex. 7 bs. 16 lb. wds. 17 nb. 40   Ex.   bs.   lb.   wds.   nb.

Total for 9 wkts. dec. 482   Total ....

FALL OF WICKETS

First Innings		Second Innings	
1	- 21	1	-
2	-142	2	-
3	-148	3	-
4	-304	4	-
5	-339	5	-
6	-430	6	-
7	-448	7	-
8	-450	8	-
9	-470	9	-

BOWLING ANALYSIS

	O	M	R	W	Wds.	NBs.	O	M	R	W	Wds.	NBs.
Lawson	37	7	114	0	9		...	...	...	...		
McDermott	36	3	141	8	7		...	...	...	...		
Holland	38	7	101	0			...	...	...	...		
O'Donnell	21	6	82	0	1		...	...	...	...		
Matthews	9	2	21	0			...	...	...	...		

LUNCH INTERVAL
1.00 - 1.40

TEA INTERVAL
3.40 - 4.00

AUSTRALIA

		First Innings		Second Innings	
1	G. R. J. MATTHEWS	b Botham	4	c & b Edmonds	17
2	A. M. J. HILDITCH	c Gower b Edmonds	49	b Emburey	40
3	K. C. WESSELS	c Botham b Emburey	34	c & b Emburey	50
* 4	A. R. BORDER	st Downton b Edmonds	8	not out	146
5	D. C. BOON	c Lamb b Botham	61	b Emburey	7
6	G. M RITCHIE	c & b Edmonds	4	b Emburey	31
† 7	W. B. PHILLIPS	c Downton b Botham	36	not out	39
0	C. J. McDERMOTT	lbw Emburey	0		
9	S. P. O'DONNELL	b Edmonds	45		
10	G. F. LAWSON	c Downton b Botham	4		
11	R. G. HOLLAND	not out	5		
12	D. R. GILBERT				

Ex. bs. 3 lb. 1 wds. 3 nb. 7   Ex. 1 bs. 6 lb. wds. 3 nb. 10

Total 257   Total for 5 wkts 340

FALL OF WICKETS

First Innings		Second Innings	
1	- 71	1	- 38
2	- 97	2	- 85
3	-118	3	-126
4	-122	4	-100
5	-193	5	-213
6	-198	6	-
7	-211	7	-
8	-223	8	-
9	-224	9	-

BOWLING ANALYSIS

	O	M	R	W	Wds.	NBs.	O	M	R	W	Wds.	NBs.
Botham	23	4	79	4	1		15	3	50	0		
Agnew	14	0	65	0	3		9	2	34	0	2	
Allott	13	1	29	0			6	2	4	0		
Emburey	24	7	41	2			51	17	99	4	1	
Edmonds	15.1	4	40	4			54	12	122	1		
Gatting							4	0	14	0		
Lamb	...	...	...	...	...	...	1	0	10	0	...	...

Umpires:
H. D. Bird & D. R. Shepherd.
*Captain †Wkt. Keeper
Scorers: A. Lowe, & M. Ringham
England won the toss & invited
Australia to bat

of the new ball. The pitch was taking a little more turn: Phillips was beaten twice in the same over and took 15 overs to get a run. But when Australia took the lead, the pressure lessened, and gradually the time–run equation became hopeless for England.

Gower played down the dropped catch, and thought the match had slipped away on Monday. 'Then there were half-a-dozen half-chances, near-chances and chances that might have been chances had someone been stood somewhere else.'

Border did his customary modest Aussie bit and praised England's spin – 'as good as I've ever faced' – and balance. He described England as 'a bloody good side'; he must know that without himself and McDermott, Australia would have looked very sorry indeed. They may have one other hero. Father Fleming of Adelaide sent the team a telegram telling them he was praying for rain. Not just lucky – it's God's own country as well.

FIFTH TEST — EDGBASTON

Monday 12 August

The England selectors, taking the Napoleonic view that unlucky players were no use to them, yesterday dropped Paul Allott for the fifth Test at Edgbaston on Thursday, and brought in Les Taylor, the 31-year-old Leicestershire fast bowler. There are no other changes.

So far this summer, bowlers have been expected to serve a one-match apprenticeship as 12th man before getting a game, and it may be that Taylor will have to stand aside to let in Richard Ellison, the 12th man at Old Trafford. However, Edgbaston is not a ground where one would expect Ellison's swing to be especially effective, and it seems most probable that on Thursday Gower will be directing Taylor and Jonathan Agnew, just as if it were Monday morning at Grace Road and the entire entertainment staged for the benefit of a few moaners in the Butler Stand.

You have to go back to Lever and Shuttleworth of Lancashire 15 years ago to find two county colleagues opening the England attack, and this development is a wonderful tribute to Leicestershire's emergence into the front rank of the English game as well as to Gower's influence on selection. It is fair to say that county batsmen do not see Leicestershire on the fixture list and immediately check on their helmets and the life insurance, but perhaps this pairing was the best available to the selectors this week.

Allott, though he did an important job in tightening the attack on the first morning at Manchester, is not taking Test wickets; Lawrence has been construed as too green; recent reports of Cowans are not encouraging; and there is doubt about the fitness and staying power of several others. Taylor, the eleventh different bowler to be named in an England twelve this season, is standing up and in form, a point emphasised by his five for 45 – including the first three batsmen for 11 – against Gloucestershire on Saturday.

Taylor is a somewhat chest-on bowler, who primarily moves the ball into the bat using seam rather than swing. His selection fits into several England traditions, old and new.

First, he is the latest and perhaps the last of the pitman fast-bowlers. He comes from the coal country near Hinckley, where the miners are as moderate as many recent England bowlers, worked on the face at the Bagworth Colliery, and took up cricket full-time only in his middle twenties, after the National Coal Board got fed up with him vanishing in the summer time.

Secondly, though he is physically very strong, his fitness record is not encouraging. Thirdly, he made his main impression on Peter May in a cup final, when he bowled very solidly in Leicestershire's Benson and Hedges win last month: get to Lord's and see the world could be the motto for aspiring England players. And fourthly, he was among the 15 who were banned for going to South Africa with Gooch's team in 1982.

Just as having been gaoled by the British is an important battle-honour in post-colonial Africa, being banned through the bleak years of '82 to '84 seems to be an asset in English cricket at the moment. Taylor is the fifth of the 15 to be chosen this summer (after Gooch, Willey, Emburey and Sidebottom), and the only one of the lot who has still not represented official England at some level.

To some cricket followers, Gooch's original dirty dozen consisted of 11 well-known players and some bloke from Leicestershire. Taylor himself seemed aware of the difference and – unlike most of his colleagues in that tour, who took the money and strolled – he bowled like a demon and made more of a name for himself than he ever had in county cricket.

Taylor himself thinks he has lost a little pace since then, but gained control. He may still have that extra bit of fire that will get Australians out. One hopes so. Time in this series is starting to run out.

The only other matter that the selectors can have discussed seriously would be the wicketkeeping, and the retention of Paul Downton was perhaps the only choice once they had decided that, even if he is a former rebel, they did not want to choose Alan

The England newcomer Les Taylor, the fourth Leicestershire player to be picked in the series and the first player to have worked at the coalface.

Knott, who will not go on tour; not on a long, official one, at any rate.

Peter May said it was a 'loyalty' decision, and compared Downton's continued selection with that of Gower and Gatting through their bad patches. I am sure Downton's form and confidence will return, and cannot offer with certainty the name of anyone except Knott who would do better. But there is a tendency for England teams to get clubby, and loyalty must be a most discouraging word for the other county 'keepers: Parks of Hampshire, for instance, is said to be having a particularly good season.

But Parks does not keep to top-class spinners, and would inevitably find it hard to adapt to Edmonds and Emburey, sight unseen, in a match as crucial as this. Sooner or later someone will emerge, and by his deeds we shall know him. In the meantime, Downton might be inspired to great things simply by hearing the name Taylor in the dressing room.

Birmingham, Thursday 15 August

For the third time this series, bad weather meant that England were unable to practise yesterday. Instead, people having business at Edgbaston on the eve of the Test were greeted by the familiar sight of Ian Botham leaving a cricket ground in a fast car and a temper, following the news that he is to appear before the TCCB disciplinary committee charged with dissent as a result of the events on the Saturday afternoon at the Trent Bridge Test.

The date of the hearing is still to be fixed though Peter May, the chairman of the selectors, hoped it would be as soon as possible. May intends to give his version of events to the committee, even though he was not on the ground at the time.

At Trent Bridge, Botham appeared in TV close-up mouthing what practised lip-readers thought just might be obscenities after a succession of decisions from umpire Alan Whitehead had gone against him.

David Gower said at the time that Whitehead had not complained to him about Botham dissenting, and it remains unclear whether Botham said anything directly to the umpire rather than the watching millions. However, Whitehead has evidently complained and the disciplinary committee will consider the case with a variety of penalties at its disposal. The most serious practicable one would be suspension. Botham has been fined twice before by cricketing authority, once for being uncomplimentary about Australian umpires and again for being uncomplimentary about the whole nation of Pakistan.

Botham's doings at least provided a diversion on yet another discouraging pre-Test Wednesday. As at Lord's and Old Trafford, the nets were too wet for England to get on, though Australia were lucky early in the day, and the pitch is thought likely to be yet another slow one, with damp at the start even if it is not – pray heaven – anything like as bad as Manchester.

There was a hint yesterday that England will not attempt to play their quickest bowler if the wicket looks unresponsive, which would mean Agnew being left out, Les Taylor making his first appearance, and Ellison (who has recovered from his cold) getting his first Test of the summer. I am dubious whether Taylor–Ellison–Botham represents an improvement on Agnew–Allott–Botham, but if Botham's foul mood can be sustained until Tuesday then anything is possible.

The weather is again rotten. The sun was shining yesterday afternoon, but there was an autumnal gale with more showers, hurrying by on the wind, forecast for today. The really bad news is that the Brumbrella, the motorised cover which Warwickshire installed with just such a match in such a summer in mind, is broken and awaiting spare parts from Finland. It could be worked manually in theory, but the club has decided to steer clear of it and rely on old technology – traditional covering and prayer.

It would be a miracle if the extraordinary Edgbaston record of seven consecutive Test finishes inside four days could be extended. But once again it seems that if a result can be achieved England have more all-round capacity, and perhaps more will, to achieve it. For some time the Australians have been thinking that they can draw here and perhaps catch England cold on a quicker surface at The Oval.

But things rarely work out quite as neatly as that, and it may be that the numbed spirit of Australia, after three such wretched months on tour, may work against them.

It is 32 years since England and Australia have gone to the last Test in this country with the destination of the Ashes still undecided, but an England win or draw here will keep this series alive to the very end. Some time within the next few days the selectors are due to name Gower as captain for the West Indies tour this winter. It could be most embarrassing if the announcement came against the background of the Ashes being lost.

FIRST DAY

Birmingham, Friday 16 August

The opening day of the fifth Test had a nasty, bitty, autumnal feel to it, as though this match were a continuation of the last, and Edgbaston a southward extension of Old Trafford. This time, however, England showed no signs of getting even a sniff of victory. Australia, put in to bat again, finished an interrupted day on 181 for two, with Wessels on 76 and Border on 43.

England missed chances against both of them, which typified a day of foul-ups of various kinds. There was one prolonged shower lasting about an hour, but no play between lunch and just before 5 pm. Had the motorised cover been functioning, the game would probably have re-started two hours earlier. The TCCB also managed to create utter confusion over the disciplining of Botham.

The one clear cut and uncontentious event was the announcement that Gower had been appointed captain for the West Indies tour this winter. I doubt if the selectors even mentioned another name – a measure of how Gower's position has strengthened since his batting form returned. One still wonders whether he is going to be a long-term captain, but this is his 19th Test in command and if he leads England simply until the end of next year – which seems highly probable – he will have done the job in more Tests than anyone except Peter May.

Gower's captaincy was less than perfect yesterday. But it was a hard day to get things right. There was a vicious cross wind buffeting everything except the ball, which kept disconcertingly straight for the England seam attack.

This consisted of Taylor, Ellison and Botham after Agnew had been left out of the 12, and Australia had decided to bring back Thomson and omit Wellham. Four Tests and endless discussion ago, the England 12 contained Cowans, Allott, Foster, and Botham; it is hard to see that we are any further forward.

As at Old Trafford, Gower, winning the toss for the third time running after losing the previous six, decided to field to take advantage of the early dampness. That was there all right, as was made obvious by the footmarks on the pitch. And it became even clearer when Edmonds came on 20 minutes before lunch and immediately found quite considerable turn.

Edmonds had already been responsible for the dismissal of Wood with a splendid diving catch at short square leg. And in his third over he put paid to Hilditch, with a classical build-up of spin before he produced the arm ball and induced a leg side nick, which Downton took well.

This was surely the moment to bring on Emburey, who could have got in two testing pre-lunch overs, with Border newly in. Instead Gower persisted with Taylor, which wasted time and an over, and it was four hours before he had a chance to make amends, by which time the pitch was a little calmer.

The innings England have long expected and feared from Wessels appears to have arrived, and he played some pleasant cover drives amid the blocking and square cutting. Border, yet again, is wearing that unstoppable look. It would take a brave man to bet against him scoring another century; every time he has passed 50 in a first-class match this tour he has done the rest.

Yet England had opportunities to capture them both. Wessels was put down three times: by Botham, most catchably, at least by his own standards, shoulder high at second slip on 13; then, more trickily, in successive late overs by Robinson at cover off Ellison and by Taylor off his own bowling.

And Border, over-balancing with only one run to his name, might have been stumped by Downton the over before lunch. Like the catch at Manchester, it was hardly more than a half chance, but in present circumstances it was enough to start speculation about how Knott might have reacted. I rather think it was too miserable a day for anyone to field at his best. It must have been hard to stand up straight, never mind play.

Among the objects being blown around with the crisp packets was the TCCB, whose officials have got into a complete muddle over Botham. On Wednesday Peter May said that Botham would be charged with dissent following his brush with umpire White-head at Nottingham. Yesterday Charles Palmer, chairman of the board, denied that a decision had been taken, while Donald Carr, the secretary, refused to confirm or deny anything. The impression created was that Botham would be charged, but that the board did not know what it was doing.

All this was an irritating sideshow on a glum day for English cricket. Almost for the first time this series the attendance was below par too, though full houses are expected today and tomorrow. There is a rumour that better weather is imminent, and another that the football season is as well. I refuse to believe either.

SECOND DAY

Birmingham, Saturday 17 August

The parameters of the second day of the Edgbaston Test were similar to those on Thursday: Cricket in the morning, nothing through a mournful afternoon, then play after tea through the extra hour to a 7 o'clock close.

However, the cricket was very different, beginning with a spectacular collapse by Australia from 189 for two to 218 for seven, followed by an equally remarkable recovery. At the end of the second day they were 335 for eight.

For the first time this series the Australians have beefed up their attack and played a non-recognised batsman at no 8; and for the first time no 8, Lawson this time, scored a 50. It is probably the best thing he has done all series. Not for the first time, it looks as though Australia have faced disaster and outstared it.

The damage to their innings was done by Richard Ellison, who marked his return to the England team with a wonderfully productive, and very well deserved, burst of four for 12 in 43 balls, and finished the day with five for 77. Ellison booked his passage to India with his performance in the penultimate Test last summer, and he may well have secured his place on this winter's tour as well.

Richard Ellison, the man of the match, whose 10 wickets impressed Fred Trueman more than the achievements of Gower and Robinson.

But this does not mean England have found the man who will silence Viv Richards at Sabina Park. This was classical English bowling on a classically English day, the sort of day that made people want to emigrate to Australia in the first place, and must have made one or two of the current Australians contemplate an immediate call to the airline.

Even in the morning, it was drizzling steadily, but the umpires kept play going, to the satisfaction of the spectators but the increasing annoyance of the Australians. In theory, cricket in the rain should hamper the fielding side most by making the ball slippery. But since the Australians were losing wickets, the water began to drip into their brains, and might have been a contributory factor in the collapse.

There might also have been sufficient rain to freshen up the pitch, which in any other circumstance would be covered. But from the start the ball was swinging and seaming far more than on the first day. I doubt if it had dried at all since the start of the match; experts on these matters were muttering about the high water table. But the wind had switched round and become less penetrating, the temperature had climbed a fraction, the ball began to drift around and Ellison used it beautifully.

Bernard Thomas, the England physio, thought Ellison was still too weak from his bout of flu last week to play at all. But Ellison was not going to miss a chance like this. He must wake up on a summer morning, see lowering clouds and, while everyone else is groaning, rub his hands with glee. Most of all, he swung the ball away from the lefthanders which is not supposed to be his forte.

He began with the most important wicket: Border, flicking to square leg, was held ankle high by Edmonds, thus maintaining his tour record of not scoring a first class 50 without going on to a hundred, but only by being out for 45.

In Ellison's next over, Wessels, on 83, was forced to play on off-stump and became Downton's 50th Test victim; Ritchie was held low down at second slip by Botham, hands for once off knees to please the sages; and then Taylor took his first England wicket by inducing an edge from O'Donnell as he tried to avoid contact.

By now the drizzle had set in, and Phillips made a big show of drying his bat handle for the umpire's benefit. His concentration had probably gone when he flashed a shorter ball to square cover.

Suddenly England were on top and the bowlers had control to an extent unknown in the first four Tests.

But that was the end of the good news. The new ball was taken, though the old one was doing very nicely. And the rain grew heavier: play was halted 10 minutes before lunch and another dismal afternoon began. There were two brief post-lunch sessions, one lasting six balls, the other 11, but that was it until 5.15.

During the evening bout of play there was one brief stoppage for bad light, in the midst of which the sun and rain returned simultaneously. The groundstaff stopped with the covers halfway to the wicket, unsure which way to go and perhaps unsure whether they ought not also ring the airline and emigrate en masse.

But it was the 11-ball session, which included an 11-run over from Botham, that set the tone for the late play. Lawson and McDermott, amateurs in this context, outshone the pros higher up the order with a carefree fightback that knocked the stuffing out of England.

Ellison got his fifth wicket: McDermott skying a catch to mid-on, which Gower judged to a nicety despite skidding and sprawling. But Ellison was tiring now. Thompson hit him for a straight six and Lawson, who had earlier received a nasty blow on the elbow from Botham, chanced what was left of his arm to great effect. Gower tried all his other main bowlers and got nowhere.

By now, the tension had gone out of the situation. Some of the crowd seemed to have taken advantage of the long stoppage to refresh themselves; a section of them near the press box were being conducted in a loud rendition of the Dam Busters. It was as puzzling as the sartorial fact that, as in the other Tests north of St John's Wood, almost everyone in the crowd seemed to be wearing a blue anorak. As a uniform, I suppose it makes more sense than MCC's egg-and-tomato tie.

THIRD DAY

Birmingham, Monday 19 August

Once again, the sow's ear summer relented to allow a silken Saturday for English cricket. If anyone had said on Friday night that there would be 355 on the scoreboard by now, you would

The great partnership: Gower and Robinson in full cry.

have assumed that Australia might have added 20 and then the rain had come back. Instead David Gower and Tim Robinson, the men of the Midlands, enraptured the crowd in the Birmingham sunshine.

In the short run, England could not possibly have asked for more. At 355 for one, already 20 ahead, their own position is impregnable and the Ashes are certain to be live at The Oval for the first time since 1953. Gower and Robinson's stand, at 317, is already England's seventh highest for any wicket against any country. The psychological dominance is complete.

The only things that went wrong all day were the fact that it took five balls rather than two to wipe out the two remaining Australian batsmen, and then the dismissal of Gooch, though no one can possibly have begrudged Thomson his 200th Test wicket, four Tests after Border dropped a sitter at Headingley and then Thomson from his team.

But, as the Irishman is supposed to have told the motorist who asked for directions: 'If I were you, sorr, I wouldn't start from here.' The game has already lost the best part of a day to bad weather. To win, England have to keep on doing everything right all through the next two days. It can happen, but the odds must still favour a second successive Australian escape.

If forced to choose for Desert Island Cricket, I would say that thus far Robinson and Gower have not quite matched Fowler and Gatting (who, despite the two double centuries, put on a mere 247 together) in the more hostile environment of Madras, last January. But it is a close-run thing.

On the Saturday of the Edgbaston Test last year, Gower failed and had a barney with a spectator as he walked in. On the same ground just 11 Saturdays ago, he got nought, lost the one-day international series, talked about dropping himself down to no 9 and saw the captaincy and his England place slipping away.

Now, captain as far as the eye can see, Gower played one of his greatest innings. He is 169 not out, having charged from 100 to 150 at a run a minute. There were some false strokes early on, a quiet period when Lawson and O'Donnell briefly tightened up the

---

A word from Thomson to mark Gower's century.

attack after lunch, and the odd uneasy moment in the nineties. But he did not give a real chance (nor did Robinson) and for most of the time was the authentic master, with his treatment of the short ball almost Richards-like in its majesty.

Robinson was Robinson. He has 140, and in ten Tests has now scored 923 runs at an average of 71. Only Bradman has played in more games and averaged better. That might not be the right comparison, but there can be no doubt that England have unearthed a player simply made for Test cricket, with the gift of turning ordinary centuries into huge ones.

A Robinson innings is a bit like all Nottinghamshire: no soaring peaks, no spectacular views, but full of fascinating bits for people with sensitivity and appreciation. He does not cover-drive exquisitely or smash sixes over the bowler's head, but he plays each ball on its merits with immense professional craft. And his skill off the back foot suggests his sequence might not necessarily come to a horrid end in the West Indies.

It must be said (and England's regular detractors will take pleasure in saying) that the bowling did not have much merit on Saturday. Though numerically stronger than in the previous four Tests, the Australian attack looks dead beat, if not indeed dead-beat: Lawson is still not right physically; McDermott kept firing the ball at Robinson's legs, which is what he would have requested; Thomson, after a decent start, kept sending down long hops and kept being hooked; Holland, though he turned a few, did so only slowly and rarely from a telling length; O'Donnell is not an international bowler.

But then the great batting records have never come against Larwood or Lillee in full cry. They have come against inadequate attacks on placid pitches; and with the moisture out of the atmosphere England were fortunate to have very much better batting conditions than Australia had. But there are already signs of scuffing that might encourage Edmonds and Emburey. Before their moment comes, England must bump up their lead, and fast. Gower agreed there was 'scope for imagination' with the batting order, which presumably means that Botham will come in next, at any rate if this pair can survive the new ball, taken just before the close on Saturday.

The establishment, which currently prefers Botha to Botham,

had a day with nothing to criticise. But Lord's finally emerged from its tangle, and announced that Botham will be arraigned before the disciplinary committee on Wednesday week to answer umpire Alan Whitehead's report from Trent Bridge. The clue to the extraordinary mess over this might just be in the wording of the charge: not just 'dissent' but 'public dissent'.

His England teammates may well say that Botham did not argue directly with Whitehead; five million TV viewers are sure that Botham swore at them. 'Call Mrs Ethel Snodgrass, of 35 Acacia Avenue. . . .'

FOURTH DAY

Birmingham, Tuesday 20 August

Only the next Atlantic depression stands this morning between England and a triumph in the Edgbaston Test that will stand comparison with any of the implausible victories of 1981. Australia, 260 behind on first innings, responded to the job of trying to save the match by crumpling to 37 for five, four of the wickets falling in 14 balls to Richard Ellison in an astonishing final half-hour.

The earlier events of the day – Gower's double hundred, Gatting's hundred, batting records galore – seemed to belong to a different game. Even Border, the second biggest irritant of England's summer, next to the weather, has gone. Ellison now has 10 wickets in the match for 79. It would be lovely to report that these last four, like the previous six, were due to excellent swing bowling. But one can only conclude that the Australians, forced to field while England piled up 595 for five, were just hopelessly demoralised.

They went in again just before 5.30. The extra hour was in play after 85 early minutes had been lost. A resultant loophole enabled the Australians to slow the over rate to 12 an hour without penalty; on a less hectic day, that might have been worth more censorious comment, but maybe Gavaskar will send Border a telegram of congratulations anyway.

Everyone here soon had other matters to consider. In the third over, Botham plugged one in short and Hilditch, who is a junkie in these matters, hooked straight to Ellison, one of the two men lying in wait. There are still people in Oxford Street who make a living playing Find the Lady, and the Australian manager ought to confiscate Hilditch's wallet whenever he goes out in London.

After that, England had some troubles. Wessels was dropped before scoring, by Emburey at slip, and some thought at the time, by Downton on 10. The customary inquests began; they were quickly adjourned.

Ellison came on from the City end. The Australians saw him and surrendered. Wessels drove at a wide one, this time definitely made contact, and Downton took it low and well. The night watchman Holland arrived, played across his first ball, was lbw and departed.

Wood tried to play to leg, and skyed to mid-wicket, giving the top three in the order a prial of 10s. Four balls later, Border was bowled off his pad and the gates to the citadel were wide open.

Yet most of the day had consisted of fagged-out bowlers being flogged all round Birmingham. Robinson passed his share of the torch to Gatting; then Gower, after seven and a half hours and 215 runs, let Lamb and, briefly and blazingly, Botham, take over.

The great partnership did not have much further to go. Two overs, and two square cut boundaries after the start, Robinson played on. He had to be content with a trivial 148, the most piffling of his three Test hundreds, and the stand turned out to be only the sixth largest in English Test history, at 331.

Gower and Robinson got past Hobbs and Rhodes to make it the second largest stand against Australia, but Hutton and Leyland remain in the pantheon, unmolested by the modern intruders. In time, perhaps, people will come to accept that Gower and Robinson and the rest of England's current batsmen are fit to be ranked close to the greats.

There can already be little argument about Gower. He became the sixth Englishman to score a double century against Australia, after Hammond, who did it four times, Hutton, R.E. Foster, Paynter and, the only post-war precedent, Barrington. It was a darn sight more entertaining than Barrington's, I can tell you, so you might say it was the best since Hutton.

At last – Robinson bowled by Lawson after $6\frac{1}{2}$ hours.

To the end, there were dodgy moments, notably on 199 when Gower hit one uppish shot, missed another, and was then hit in the euphemisms. And after 200, it seemed as though he was trying to get out to bring in Botham, while the Australians were trying to keep him in and Botham at bay. Gower was dropped twice before Border took him.

Gower had agreed on Saturday that there was 'scope for imagination' over the batting order. And in mid-afternoon, with the ball ageing and the bowlers likewise, that could only mean Botham, couldn't it? Instead, Lamb appeared as per programme. It hardly mattered, since Gatting was now in full cry and Lamb matched him: They put on 73 in the 13 overs before tea. And if this was an example of Gower's occasional Hamlet tendencies as a captain, his batting was enough like a sweet Prince for him to be forgiven almost anything.

His own career best, 200 against India here six years ago, and Compton's record of 562 in a home series against Australia fell to Gower almost incidentally, though a few weeks ago he sat in this pavilion and wondered where the next run might come from, never mind the next 215.

Botham eventually emerged when Lamb was out almost two hours later. It was a compact innings; 18 runs, seven balls, of which the first and third went for sixes off McDermott, over long on and into the pavilion – his 75th and 76th in the first class cricket this summer and his 100th and 101st adding in one-day games as well. He holed out to deep mid-wicket, where Thomson took the catch and gave the spectators a little gesture of the sort to which Botham himself has on occasion been prone when things were going badly for him.

Gower declared after Gatting had completed his fourth Test hundred in nine months. It had been an innings of dash, flair, and immense confidence. But the statistics were now coming in like autumn leaves into the gutter and it was hardest of all to remember how once we had despaired of him. The final stages of the day were even more breathtaking. At the close, the evening sun was casting long, optimistic shadows. If that priest in Adelaide is praying for rain again, the massed ranks of English clerics should get together and shout him down.

FIFTH DAY

Birmingham, Wednesday 21 August

England beat Australia and an even older and, on this occasion, far more formidable adversary, the weather, to win the fifth Test at Edgbaston yesterday.

In an atmosphere of extraordinary tension, which affected everyone except Jim Laker, commentating as phlegmatically as ever on television, England bowled out Australia for 142 in the ninth over of the final 20 to win by an innings and 118 runs. It was their biggest victory in an Ashes Test since the match in which Laker himself took 19 wickets at Old Trafford in 1956.

However, Allan Border, the Australian captain, was very bitter about the day's most vital decision, when Wayne Phillips was given out, caught by Gower, after the ball had ricocheted off Allan Lamb's foot.

Umpire David Shepherd consulted his colleague David Constant before giving Phillips out, but Border was convinced the ball had struck the ground first.

'I was very, very disappointed with the decision. There's no way in the world they could tell that was out.' Gower called Constant courageous and said all his close fielders were sure the umpire was right.

For much of the day, an England win looked improbable. The first three hours were lost to rain, and then Phillips and Greg Ritchie put together a stand of 81. But Phillips' dismissal set off another collapse, and the last five wickets fell in 47 minutes.

England now go to the Oval a week tomorrow for the sixth and final Test leading 2–1 in the series. They will regain the Ashes, lost in Australia in 1982/3 as long as they can avoid defeat.

When everyone is a little calmer, Edgbaston 1985 will go down as both a tremendous England triumph and an epic Test match. After the game, Border created a substantial diversion by complaining about the dismissal of Phillips; in time I suspect everyone will come to see that as an irrelevance and a rather ill-judged one.

There were only 65 balls left when England won by an innings

Cornhill Insurance

N⁰ 6 TOTAL N⁰ 5
1   37   0
WICKETS 5
LAST PLAYER   2
9 BOWLERS   10
2 1 OVERS FLD.
LAST WKT FFU

The scoreboard that taunted England – and Ellison above all – through a damp Tuesday morning when it looked as though Australia might escape.

and 118 runs. But this had little to do with the Australians. Even England in their darkest moments of the past few years have hardly been outplayed quite as spectacularly as Australia have been since Saturday morning.

The weather was England's only serious adversary. But the weather did not whinge afterwards, though the wind howled and tried to blow down the sightscreen. Border did whinge. And it was both bizarre and unfortunate that after such a crushing defeat the Australians should not just be reflecting that God is, after all, an Englishman, but that the umpires are Englishmen too.

The dismissal of Phillips was the critical moment of the shortened fifth day, though hardly of the match. Phillips, who had spent most of the afternoon crashing the ball through the offside close field, tried it again. This time it ricocheted off Lamb's instep

The catch which Border thought turned the match (*opposite and above*): Phillips on the back foot ... Lamb pirouettes ... and parries to Gower who claims the wicket ... and gets it from umpire Shepherd after consultation with Constant. 113 for six.

(that is not in doubt; the instep was in ice last night) as he took evasive action and Gower snatched the rebound.

Umpire Shepherd was unsighted and uncertain; he went over to Constant at square leg, who had no doubts. 'We didn't deserve to get out of the match but the decision cost us it,' Border said. 'Phillips told me he hit it into the ground. If Constant was right, he was guessing. He must have been obscured by the close fielders. England's umpires are the best in the world, but one of them made a bit of a blue today.'

Border says he has seen the replay 20 times and is sure it was not out. Not everyone agrees, including this observer. But it does seem a peculiarly fatuous issue over which to raise such a storm. If Constant had given an obviously bad decision and Australia had lost by 18 runs, it would be fair enough. But it cannot seriously be called more than doubtful; the umpire raised his finger and Australia lost by an innings and 118. Border should have kept quiet; and this morning I expect he will see that himself.

That wicket ended the second of the day's three phases. The first was the familiar one as the rain lashed Edgbaston, at times horizontally. People will not believe how nostalgic you can get on tour at Madras or Melbourne for a real English November day. And now we had one, on August 20, with the scoreboard tauntingly reading Australia 37 for 5. One began to think of past great Australian escapes: Manchester '53, Lord's '68. . . .

ENGLAND WON BY
AN INNINGS &
118 RUNS.

England v. Australia
FIFTH TEST MATCH
at Edgbaston
August 15, 16, 17, 19, & 20, 1985

ENGLAND

MAN OF THE MATCH R.M. ELLISON.

		First Innings			Second Innings
1. G.A. GOOCH	(ESSEX)	c Phillips b Thomson	19		
2. R.T. ROBINSON	(NOTTS.)	b Lawson	148		
*3. D.I. GOWER	(LEICS.)	c Border b Lawson	215		
4. M.W. GATTING	(MIDDLESEX)	Not Out	100		
5. A.J. LAMB	(NORTHANTS)	c Wood b McDermott	46		
6. I.T. BOTHAM	(SOMERSET)	c Thomson b McDermott	18		
+7. P.R. DOWNTON	(MIDDLESEX)	Not Out	0		
8. J.E. EMBUREY	(MIDDLESEX)				
9. R.M. ELLISON	(KENT)				
10. P.H. EDMONDS	(MIDDLESEX)				
11. L.B. TAYLOR	(LEICS.)				
		Extras	49	Extras	
		Total	595 – 5 dec.	Total	

Fall of wickets - First Innings 1- 38 2- 369 3- 463 4- 572 5- 592 6- 7- 8- 9- 10-
Second Innings 1- 2- 3- 4- 5- 6- 7- 8- 9- 10-

Bowling Analysis 1st Innings	O	M	R	W	2nd Innings	O	M	R	W
LAWSON	37	1	135	2					
McDERMOTT	31	2	155	2					
THOMSON	19	1	101	1					
HOLLAND	25	4	95	0					
O'DONNELL	16	3	69	0					
BORDER	6	1	13	0					

AUSTRALIA

		First Innings			Second Innings	
1. G.M. WOOD	(W. AUSTRALIA)	c Edmonds b Botham	19	c R'son b Ellison	10
2. A.M.J. HILDITCH	(S. AUSTRALIA)	c Downton b Edmonds	39	c Ellison b Botham	10
3. K.C. WESSELS	(QUEENSLAND)	c Downton b Ellison	83	c Downton b Ellison	10
4. A.R. BORDER	(QUEENSLAND)	c Edmonds b Ellison	45	b Ellison	2
5. G.M. RITCHIE	(QUEENSLAND)	c Botham b Ellison	8	c Lamb b Emburey	20
6. W.B. PHILLIPS	(S. AUSTRALIA)	c Robinson b Ellison	15	c Gower b Emburey	59
7. S.P. O'DONNELL	(VICTORIA)	c Downton b Taylor	1	b Botham	11
8. G.F. LAWSON	(N.S. WALES)	Run Out	53	c Gower b Edmonds	3
9. C.J. McDERMOTT	(QUEENSLAND)	c Gower b Ellison	35	c Edmonds b Botham	8
10. J.R. THOMSON	(QUEENSLAND)	Not Out	28	Not Out	4
11. R.G. HOLLAND	(N.S. WALES)	c Edmonds b Ellison	0	lbw b Ellison	0
		Extras	9	Extras	5
		Total	335	Total	142

Fall of wickets - First Innings 1- 44 2- 92 3- 189 4- 191 5- 207 6- 208 7- 218 8- 276 9- 335 10- 335
Second Innings 1- 10 2- 32 3- 32 4- 35 5- 36 6- 113 7- 117 8- 120 9- 137 10- 142

Bowling Analysis 1st Innings	O	M	R	W	2nd Innings	O	M	R	W
BOTHAM	27	1	108	1	BOTHAM	14.1	2	52	3
TAYLOR	26	5	78	1	TAYLOR	13	4	27	0
ELLISON	31.5	9	77	6	ELLISON	9	3	27	4
EDMONDS	20	4	47	1	EDMONDS	15	9	13	2
EMBUREY	9	2	21	0	EMBUREY	13	5	19	1

* Captain   + Wicketkeeper   Scorers: S.P. AUSTIN. M.P. RINGHAM.   Umpires: D.J. CONSTANT. D.R. SHEPHERD.   Toss won by:- ENGLAND WHO ELECTED TO FIELD.

NEW BALL:: the fielding team may not claim a new ball until 85 overs have been bowled.
HOURS OF PLAY : 11.00 am - 6.00 pm (or after 90 overs bowled whichever is the later).   LUNCH : 1.00 pm - 1.40 pm TEA : 3.40 pm.

Lamb (hidden behind stumps) clings on at silly point and Ritchie is out. 117 for seven.

The rain gave over. An announcement said that play would start at 2.0; immediately it rained again. At 2.30 play did start; two balls later it stopped – the rain was back. Ten minutes after that the players returned and this time there were no more interruptions, but England had lost the magic of Monday night.

Ellison could get nowhere, and Phillips got on to the back foot to punch the ball through the packed offside. It was a dangerous tactic, especially when Botham returned and bowled quite magnificently with eight men on the off, like a football wall. He got nowhere; maybe he should have tried lolloping long hops with a legside trap.

Finally forty minutes after tea Edmonds (or Constant, if you are Australian) made the breakthrough. Then Emburey turned one a fraction into Ritchie, and Lamb snapped up a close offside catch. And off the fourth ball of the final twenty overs Lawson went to a second-attempt catch by Gower, who, amid the array of close fielders, would have to be described as very silly point.

O'Donnell and McDermott resisted for the next six overs. At first, Gower stuck with the spinners. But Botham was 'champing at the bit' (Gower's phrase). Off came Edmonds, on came Botham, out went O'Donnell, bowled through the gate – Botham's 129th Australian Test victim, beating Willis's record.

At the start of Botham's next over, McDermott edged to forward short leg. The last five wickets had fallen for 29, seven fewer than the first five, and only the Phillips-Ritchie stand had saved Australia from one of their lowest ever scores. It was all over bar the bitching.

A bowler, Fred Trueman, was picking the man of the match, and Ellison's 10 for 104 beat Gower's 215. Gower will have the slightly more important prize of the Ashes, just as long as England avoid losing at the Oval. On current form, one would expect England to make a reasonable contest of it with the weather to see whether it can be 3-1. The Australians, unless they make a remarkable recovery, appear to be the least of England's worries.

McDermott is caught at short leg. England have won, and Botham is quite pleased.

SIXTH TEST — THE OVAL

Twenty-four hours after his team lost the Edgbaston Test, the Australian manager, Bob Merriman, was dragged along to a London nightclub on some spurious pretext only to discover his players emerging from corners to give him a surprise birthday party.

It was, by all accounts, quite a night. Wayne Phillips played the piano – he is said to know three bars of The Sting – while Simon O'Donnell and Allan Border sang, though they are slightly less musically accomplished. Most remarkable of all, everyone behaved decorously.

In the 70s, whenever the Australians held a party like that, air raid warnings had to be issued over a wide area. This time most of the wives were present, and the one person who was disgusted by events was the pianist who had been hired for the evening only to find herself unappreciated. The standard of Australian musicianship, as well as batsmanship, has declined since the days when Bradman provided triple centuries and piano medleys.

The jollity was just a little forced. The Australians feel beaten now. They can save the Ashes by winning at The Oval and – remembering their habit of being at their most dangerous when most reviled – that cannot be ruled out. But there was not a soul this week, English or Australian, who seriously believed it would happen.

The Australians go into their match at Canterbury today with selection policy in utter confusion. Wellham, Gilbert and Bennett, who have not yet played a Test this tour, are now all major contenders. Wellham was ignored all through the 1981 series, then came in and made a hundred at The Oval. England, meanwhile, can seriously contemplate an unchanged 12.

For English cricket, the good news gets better. Advance bookings for The Oval are phenomenal. If you want to go on the first three days, forget it. There are just a few £8 tickets left for Monday.

Receipts for the Tests and one-day Internationals are now around £2.9 million, way, way ahead of any previous figures. The game has survived the raindance summer almost bone-dry, despite, or maybe because of, the scheme of offering advance purchasers their money back if there is no play. County treasurers are moaning about the effects of the weather on Cheltenham and Canterbury and such like, but the cheque from headquarters will be a very handsome compensation.

This will be cricket's fifth fat year in succession, though it could hardly have been wetter. Those of us who believe the game is in danger of over-selling itself and, in particular, overtaxing its participants, had, I suppose, better keep quiet for a moment.

There are a few people who ought to have kept quieter this week. Border's post-Test outburst about the dismissal of Wayne Phillips looks no better with the passage of time.

Some people were not surprised about it. The diplomatic arts have not come naturally to Border, but he has done a stupendous job throughout an exceptionally difficult tour, made harder by the defections to South Africa at the start, the constant undercurrent created by that, the crummy weather and the pressure of being the best player in an inferior side, which for $4\frac{1}{2}$ Tests held on. There is a limit to the amount of grace under pressure anyone can show, and Border cracked. He has still been a quite outstanding touring captain.

But already one senses a mood that the decisive moment has passed; the Australians are probably going to remember it as the War of Lamb's Boot. It is a very dangerous mood indeed for England, but already thoughts are turning to winter and the contest against Viv Richards's Empire of the Sun. This brings in the week's other unfortunate set of comments, from the Antiguan prime minister Lester Bird, whose appearance on BBC's Newsnight set off another frisson of doubt about whether the tour can take place.

Bird's line of thought was at least more carefully thought through than the 'No regrets' interview Graham Gooch gave to the BBC which induced them. Bird now wants a threefold statement from Gooch deploring apartheid, stating his intention not to

return to South Africa as long as apartheid exists, and an expression of regret. He wrote to Lord's along these lines before leaving town. The official TCCB line is that they will demand no such statement, though if Gooch wants to make one he can do so. They would, I think, prefer Gooch to clear it with them first.

There is, no doubt, an element of grandstanding in Bird's position. Antigua has a similar population to Worcester and its politicians do not get invited to appear on Newsnight to discuss the prospects for this year's yam crop. I think there was a touch of pique, too. The Antiguans feel they played a major part in getting the Caribbean heads of government to agree, at a meeting last February, that the recently banned players should be admitted. And Gooch's comments were seen as a betrayal.

It is all barmy, as has been said here before. Gooch's political views are his affair, a promise not to return is, of course, worthless, and, anyway, how do you define apartheid in this context? But at first sight, these two should not be a problem. Regret might be.

Here, the Antiguans have kindly left a loophole. What Bird requires is 'regret of the circumstances which compelled Gooch to South Africa'. It really ought to be possible for someone to cobble up a statement to encompass that. Of course Gooch thinks the circumstances were regrettable – cricketers should earn more money in the first place.

The Antiguan High Commissioner in London, Ronald Sanders, said yesterday: 'I don't think we have given any thought to the possibility that Gooch will not make this statement.'

Antigua wants the tour to go on: Richards leading a team in his home country is not a negligible matter of national pride. But it can manage without. The country has legal gaming and a large marina; it can fill its hotel beds very nicely without any help from the England cricket team and their attendants. And one can already detect some uneasy shuffling among the other Caribbean countries. If Antigua were to ban Gooch, others might quickly follow; no one wants to be seen as soft on apartheid, however absurd or irrelevant the test case.

The message, though, appears to be don't panic and perhaps,

Bob Merriman, the Australian manager, at a thought-provoking moment in the series.

to both Gooch and Border, when in doubt say nowt. One is reluctant to mention that. The game needs people who will speak their minds, instead of being permanently in a meeting or in the dressing room. Best, however, if they engage brain first.

Monday 26 August

The England selectors yesterday did the decent thing and named an unchanged squad to face Australia in the final Test this week. The 11 heroes of Edgbaston, together with the twelfth man Jonathan Agnew, will reassemble at The Oval on Wednesday afternoon, provided Ian Botham has not been incarcerated in some Lord's dungeon after his disciplinary hearing in the morning.

The selectors took two hours to take the decision, in which time they chewed over events at Edgbaston but did not, apparently, look forward to the winter tour. Since we can safely assume that Peter May did not spend the meeting jumping up and down and crying 'Yippie' (though there was every reason to do so), there must have been considerable discussion about the fast bowling and Agnew in particular.

It would have been unjust to leave out Agnew on the grounds that he has not done much lately. There is not much he can do if he spends his life carrying drinks or watching the rain. But one gets the impression that Agnew has been kept on for negative, Bedserish there's-no-one-else reasons.

Both Agnew and Les Taylor will probably need a good game at The Oval to get to the West Indies, yet one or other is the most likely twelfth man (Agnew will presumably play if the wicket looks at all fast, Taylor if not).

Even if the question of tour places was not formally discussed, a few trends are emerging: Cowans and Dilley appear to be edging back into favour; Foster, though he has again only played one Test all summer, has never really been out of it. However, the squad will not be announced until September 20, and the picture could look very different by then.

Nothing else can have bothered the selectors. The hounds are no longer baying quite so loudly for Downton's blood; the spinners have no serious rivals; the batting looks magnificent. If no one is injured before Thursday, it will be the first time England's top six has played unchanged through a full length series since, well, actually, since the days of Fowler, Robinson, Gatting, Gower, Lamb and Cowdrey in India last winter; but it does seem to be unprecedented at home.

The hard bit with the batting will come when the tour party is picked and only one or two others of a very large crowd of worthies can clamber aboard. Chris Broad is again being talked about as a reserve opener, Wilf Slack's consistency is at last getting the notice it deserves (but ye gods, SIX Middlesex players?); and word of Worcestershire's David Smith relish for fast bowling has moved up the line. But, inevitably, there are going to be some very unlucky batsmen indeed.

England have already filled one crucial if unsung role for the winter and perhaps the future. Laurie Brown, the 44-year-old Lancashire physiotherapist, has been chosen to accompany the team to the Caribbean in succession to Bernie Thomas.

Brown is a Scot who makes no pretence to technical cricket expertise. But he spent 12 years with Manchester United and so knows a lot about the physio's role on an overseas trip: this includes massaging egos as well as backs, arguing with stroppy hotel clerks and baggage handlers, and generally acting as prop and helpmeet to the manager and the whole party. Thomas was a particular genius with prematch exercises, ingrown toenails and Indian hucksters.

Before the players can even contemplate the tour, though, Australia must be despatched. But now, with England 2–1 up, any rain will be batting for them rather than the Australians.

Whatever the weather there is now a firm belief that the Ashes will be back here a week tomorrow.

The Oval, Thursday 29 August

There was at least one calm place in cricket yesterday afternoon: in The Oval nets 12 of the 13 members of the England party went through their time-honoured motions and the Chairman of Selectors made time-honoured pre-Test remarks.

Everything was happening around them. On the perimeter of the ground, workmen did fearfully noisy things with chainsaws in preparation for what is almost certainly the only Test in this country for which the first four days have all been sold out in advance.

Across the Harleyford Road other workmen put up Lambeth Council anti-Thatcher slogans which may not have much effect on the Government but will scare the living daylights out of the BBC producer.

Meanwhile, in another part of the wood, Ian Botham faced, and evidently outfaced, the Lord's disciplinary committee which, after 4½ hours, decided merely to slap his wrists for his behaviour on the Saturday of the Trent Bridge Test. Botham walked rather than limped away, and there was some optimism that his knee injury, in traditional Botham style, will have recovered in time for him to start the final Test this morning.

Even farther away, in the West Indies, politicians digested the statement from Graham Gooch repudiating apartheid and another tour of South Africa. Lester Bird, the Foreign Minister of Antigua who had insisted on the statement, said Gooch would now be persona grata; and there seems no further obstacle to the winter Caribbean tour going ahead.

Whether England go there in possession of the Ashes seems a more open question than it did a few days ago, although at least the TCCB did not attempt to ban Botham from today's game.

The disciplinary committee, chaired temporarily by Charles Palmer (the regular chairman Colin Atkinson stood down because of his Somerset connections); considered evidence from the umpires, David Gower and Botham and watched videos of the Third Test. Then they found that Botham had shown 'considerable frustration and an element of dissent amounting to misconduct on the field, which the Committee felt would bring the game into disrepute'.

Botham was reprimanded and warned that any repetition would be likely to have 'serious repercussions'. However, the absence of immediate repercussions suggest that Botham and his lawyer have won a victory of sorts over umpire Alan Whitehead, who reported him.

Perhaps the punishment or lack of it will inspire Botham to put mind over ligaments and make a super-human effort to be fit. It is hard to imagine an occasion like this – an Ashes decider with every seat sold – with him on the sidelines. It is even harder to imagine Bill Athey, called into the squad late on Tuesday as standby, as an adequate replacement.

Peter May admitted as much yesterday. His thinking was that since there is no substitute for Botham, it was best, with England 2–1 up, to choose a specialist batsman and, if the worst comes to the worst, use Gooch as the third seamer.

However, the choice of Athey does reflect the selectors' old habit of picking players just after they have run out of form. In July, Athey was playing well. In August, he is averaging 11 from eight first class innings; that is slightly better than his Test average of 2.83 from six innings. Of course, neither figure reflects Athey's considerable talent. But really: poor old Randall, they just won't have him, will they?

Suddenly the Australians have fewer selection problems. They have dropped the old stagers, Thomson and Holland and, like Randall, it is hard to see either playing Test cricket again. Except for the reserve wicketkeeper, Ray Phillips, all the members of the touring team who have not played in the previous five Tests are included in their 12: Dave Gilbert, the fast bowler, Murray Bennett, the slow left-armer and Dirk Wellham, the batsman who made a century when he was brought in for his debut on this ground, are in and Bennett and Gilbert look sure to play. The last place appears to rest between Wellham and Simon O'Donnell, who has not quite made the grade either as batsman or bowler.

Everything, of course, depends on the pitch. Harry Brind, the groundsman, is delighted with the preparation. Somehow he has kept it as dry as he wanted, and it looks and feels far firmer than anything the Australians have seen all tour. London even had a touch of Sydney heat yesterday, as though we were nearing the end of a proper August.

In spite of our climate, we are a kindly nation. With England 2–1 up, the Australians might have expected a surface as dreary as Trent Bridge. Whether or not it matches the amazingly pacey wicket Brind produced for the New Zealand Test in 1983, conditions are bound to feel less alien to the Australians than they have done. The Ashes, for England, are still five very hard days' work away.

FIRST DAY

The Oval, Friday 30 August

On a brilliant day of high summer and high batsmanship, Graham Gooch and David Gower effectively regained the Ashes for England at The Oval yesterday, and knocked out of the 1985 Australians whatever stuffing they might have had left.

The day began with a triumph for Craig McDermott and finished with a wicket maiden for Murray Bennett, but in between Gooch and Gower caused utter mayhem. At the close England were 376 for three, Gooch was still there with 179, Gower was out for 157. They put on 351 for the second wicket, the Gower–Robinson stand of 331 at Edgbaston being passed as the sixth highest in English Test history after just 10 days.

There are other mind-blowing statistics. But Gower and Gooch did not beat the kind of record people normally trot out on routine days – the highest for the second wicket for England against Australia on this ground. The Hutton and Leyland stand of 382 in 1938 still reigns supreme.

That match (England 903 for seven declared, Hutton 364) is usually regarded as the apogee of English batting. But it was achieved against a weaker Australian seam attack than this, at a time when Australia had already won the Ashes, and was scored far more slowly. England, having kept up a remarkable 3.6 an over all series, were above four an over yesterday.

It would take a very committed fogey to insist that the performances of Gower and company this summer do not rank among the all-time great English batting feats. And there has surely never been a series when England's batsmen have so dominated Australia's bowlers; what people thought would be the great confrontation of force versus object has been wholly one-sided since Lord's.

The first good news of the day for England yesterday was that Botham was fit, and the team was left unchanged. I am still not certain they were right to do without Agnew, but Botham was irrelevant yesterday, so Agnew certainly was. What did matter was Border calling wrong for the fourth Test running (it must be Gower's 10-franc coin again) and allowing England to take first strike on a pitch as dry and fair as the groundsman, Harry Brind, had promised.

Australia's bowlers might have been able to use the pace to trouble England. And Robinson, missing out for once, soon lost his off stump to an in-swinging yorker from McDermott. But their reshaped team soon proved as inadequate in these conditions as they were on the slow pitches of Manchester and Birmingham.

ENGLAND'S HIGHEST TEST PARTNERSHIPS

411	P. B. H. May and M. C. Cowdrey	4th wicket v.	West Indies, Edgbaston 1957
382	L. Hutton and M. Leyland	2nd wicket v.	Australia, The Oval 1938
370	W. J. Edrich and D. C. S. Compton	3rd wicket v.	South Africa, Lord's 1947
369	J. H. Edrich and K. F. Barrington	2nd wicket v.	New Zealand, Headingley 1965
359	L. Hutton and C. Washbrook	1st wicket v.	South Africa, Johannesburg 1948–49
351	G. A. Gooch and D. I. Gower	2nd wicket v.	Australia, The Oval 1985
331	D. I. Gower and R. T. Robinson	2nd wicket v.	Australia, Edgbaston 1985
323	J. B. Hobbs and W. Rhodes	1st wicket v.	Australia, Melbourne 1911–12

McDermott, straining for more yorkers, soon began producing half-volleys, and Lawson, alas for Australia, continued weary and sickly, if staunch. The newcomer, Gilbert, bowled straight, and Gooch drove him straighter, while the slow left-armer, Bennett looked a very slow left-armer indeed. With the ball not turning, he was cannon fodder.

But it could have been different. Gower began as though the weird sisters had said that no harm would befall him until St John's Wood come to Kennington. Most of the shots in his first 50 were speculative, and he might have been caught in the slips on two and on 31, though the only chance that actually went to hand or finger was one to Wessels at cover on 137.

After lunch – perhaps the captain had had a word with himself

Gooch and Gower, as they pass Gower and Robinson's huge stand. Gooch, assured, never gave the opposition a hope until he was out for 196; Gower, through his first 50, played in curiously speculative fashion.

– he was as majestic as at Edgbaston, playing every shot you could wish for (except the reverse sweep) until, tired, he slashed to backward point after 5½ hours. By then Gower had taken his total for the series to 732, the fourth highest by an Englishman (behind Hammond, 905, Compton, 753, and Sutcliffe, 734). I think I can say with some certainty that it is the highest total by a batsman who was as dispirited and as close to the plug hole as Gower was only three months ago.

Gooch did not give a chance. He already has his first Ashes century, after 14 frustrating games, and his highest Test score. This morning, perhaps, he will have a double century.

And one trusts no one will demand an apology and a promise not to do it again. He mixed power with delicacy; his sweeps against poor Bennett had touches of impertinence. After tea, when he finally moved convincingly ahead of Gower, Gooch looked unstoppable. Maybe the new Hutton is amongst us.

There were several symbolic moments. After one Gower hook McDermott simply stood and stared hopelessly at the ground for ages. Later the Fosters balloon, which looked the weediest of the

---

The England total mounts . . . and so do the unofficial banners. Alcohol vies with land rights and London politics.

various advertising stunts attempted by competing Australian lagers, broke loose from its moorings to become a hazard to aviation, and the fielders stared as if hoping to hitch a ride. Then a group of pigeons waddled across the pitch on a fast bowler's length, perhaps imagining that it was the safest route.

Even the good news had a bad side for Australia. In the last over Bennett turned one past the outside edge of Gatting's bat and induced a slip catch. It brought in Emburey as night watchman. Gatting and Robinson thus become analogous to Edrich, Compton and Paynter, who made 13 between them in Hutton's match. But turn, with England 376 for three? Emburey should have gone to bed last night almost as happily as the day's two heroes.

SECOND DAY

The Oval, Saturday 31 August

It was gloriously sunny again at The Oval yesterday, but with a sultry edge suggesting that the weather will be reverting to 1985 type before the weekend is out.

The unaccustomed heat must be getting to the players: the final Test has veered off in an unexpected direction. England finished the second day on top, as they started it, but not at all in the manner anyone imagined.

Up to 6.15 on Thursday only one wicket had fallen in this match; just after six yesterday, Wayne Phillips was the 16th man out and Australia, who at one stage must have wondered whether they might still be fielding this afternoon, were already in danger of the follow-on. England were all out for 464, and the vital figure for Australia is 265. At the close they were 145 for six.

Yet the early part of the day had belonged entirely to them. England, having been 371 for one, before Gower was out, and 376 for three overnight, lost their last nine wickets for 93. As at Trent Bridge last month, the batsmen climbed halfway up the mountainside then ran out of oxygen.

There was no double century for Gooch; he was out in the fourth over of the day for 196, equalling Border's score at Lord's. After Gower's 157 and the 50 extras (the Australians kindly donated 32 no-balls, including those scored off) the next highest contribution was Downton's 16. But the Australians failed even to build a position from which they could collapse. The batsmen departed at regular intervals throughout the afternoon. Emburey and Edmonds began to get dry turn; Ellison swung the ball; Botham was Botham.

If there was a pattern, other than dog-day insanity, it may lie in the way the lefthanders, Wessels, Border, and Phillips, all lost stumps trying to play the spinners away on the off side, a technique which has brought all three plenty of runs on the slower pitches of the first five Tests, but brought only disaster with the extra pace and bounce here. So far only Gooch and Gower have proved adaptable enough to cope with the sudden change.

The bowling, it must be said, was dramatically better all round than on Thursday. Australia took the new ball at the start, and this time did not waste it. Lawson, looking less put-upon than of late, and McDermott bowled a decent line at a fair lick, and the match was transformed.

Admittedly it was a full toss that had Gooch, who had taken another 17 off the first three overs, caught and bowled after seven hours. But then Lawson (whose Test record this month had read two for 327 at the start of play) had a burst of three for three. The nightwatchman, Emburey, cut to point, and Lamb, with two long legs, proceeded to hook – which would make him the soppiest ha-porth on either side if the Australians, as I shall relate, did not have a soppier one.

Botham played 22 balls with great seriousness and much shouldering of arms and ducking of bouncers. He was not going to fall into the hook trap. No sir. He drove firm-footed instead, and was caught behind.

The others went quietly and Border, who late on Thursday would probably have given a minor limb to get England out for under 500, led a triumphant Australia back to the dressing room. The bookmaker who had offered 100–1 against them in the morning now looked a little over-generous. But England had still passed 450 for the fifth Test out of six, and if Gooch and Gower had not so over-inflated expectations would have been well pleased.

They were soon happy again. Botham started it, of course. The *Sun* had dressed him up for a picture stunt that was inane even

Lamb falls for the baited hook, in more ways than one. McDermott took the catch at long-leg.

by prevailing standards and rechristened him Rambotham, which makes him sound like a town in Lancashire. But he probably sees the Ashes as his private war, beyond logic, and after getting Wood lbw (to some raised eyebrows, as it might have been missing off stump), he bowled to Hilditch.

Now Hilditch is the Australian vice-captain and a lawyer, both of which pre-suppose something up top. But he is also rather like a greyhound, never cottoning on that the hare is fake. Two long legs, short ball, compulsive hook, on your bike – just as at Edgbaston. Unbelievable.

Wessels tried to cut and was out to Emburey for the sixth time in the series; Wellham was done by Ellison's outswinger; Border, to England's special delight, inside edged against Edmonds, who also bowled Phillips as he hit against the spin.

By the end only Ritchie, of the recognised batsmen, was left,

Friday night delight for England: Phillips is bowled by Edmonds.

and Australia still needed 120 to avoid the follow-on. The pitch is not going to turn less as it grows older. England failed in their first objective yesterday – an unbeatable score. I don't know though: perhaps they are now so cocky that it was all tactical, an attempt to get Australia out twice before the weather turns nasty again.

THIRD DAY

The Oval, Monday 2 September

Sometime today, or tomorrow at the latest, the Ashes will return to England, having departed hence at the end of the Sydney Test in January 1983 – at least if you believe cricket's guiding myth and not the reality in the Lord's museum.

Australia, forced to follow on by England, will start the fourth day at 62 for four, still 161 behind. A combination of Border, Ritchie, Phillips and September will have to do something fairly bloody-minded to stop England going 3–1 up in the series. An Australian win to keep the Ashes is hardly even a measurable risk.

On Saturday night Allan Border publicly waved the flag of surrender. He was serene now, and there was no grieving at the umpiring, or anything else.

The Oval pitch was exactly what Australia had wanted. The toss had made no difference, as he thought their best chance had been to get England in and try and take quick wickets. He agreed that 3–1 would probably be a fair reflection of the series. It was a bit like listening to Walter Mondale's concession speech.

'The fight goes on,' said Border. 'But obviously we're not in a real good position. I look back on Headingley '81 and think maybe the good Lord will send something down for me one day.'

Headingley '81! The *leitmotiv* of the series has come back to haunt the closing stages as it haunted the start. Sometimes people get over-obsessed with that match. There was criticism of Gower on Saturday for making Australia bat again on the grounds that he had given Australia their one slender chance of winning.

This seems to me fearfully wet, like walking through Kennington worrying about being charged by a rhino. The Test is there to be won as well as the Ashes. The argument is fallible too, since it is based on the hypothesis that England might bat terribly, though if they are going to bat badly on Tuesday, why should they not also bat badly on Saturday? Australia, remember, have only one real spinner. Gower took the bolder course, and it looks as if he will be rewarded.

As Border seems to have recognised, Australia lost the series and their bottle at Edgbaston, and everything that has happened in this Test is merely commentary. A cricket tour is a hard slog, and this has been harder than most.

Since the end of the Packer split, only the West Indians, of course, and England – in India last winter – have won a major overseas series. And the Australians (the tyranny of distance, perhaps, as well as the tyranny of the current fixture list) have proved worse travellers than most. If they lose this Test, their away record, going back to the start of Packer in May 1977, will be played

44, won five, lost 22. In England the record will be played 17, won two, lost nine.

Border suggested a shorter tour with the big matches spread out more (though I dare say the Australians would moan if they had less time to acclimatise) and a return to five Tests which would satisfy every demand except the game's growing avarice.

Border also looked ahead with a shudder to the press conference he will shortly have to give at Sydney Airport. 'It's going to be very hard to convince people that we really do have a lot of promising young players,' he sighed.

Cricketing success goes in cycles. Even as the West Indians were putting the finishing touches to the blackwash 12 months ago, it was possible to predict that 1985, with England back at full strength and Australia in search of a new generation, might be a year when the Ashes came home. Clive Lloyd, in his triumphal press conference at The Oval, praised the vanquished Gower, said he was the right man for the job, and suggested that he would soon prove it.

One's confidence in England's ability to beat Australia this summer wavered only briefly – at the start of the tour when, momentarily, the fast bowling looked really good: when Thomson (at Taunton) produced his best-ever bowling in England; when Lawson's indispositions looked temporary; and when McDermott was making his first impression.

At that stage, some Australian observers thought this team might be like that of 1972, when a young side unexpectedly drew 2-2 with England (as they still could this year if pigs grow wings) before Thomson joined Lillee and created the basis for the storming team of the mid-70s.

But the Australians are not a nation of especially good losers. And the danger now is that they will start to think wistfully of the 16 who have defected to South Africa and imagine that they would have made the difference.

Kim Hughes will seem like a lost leader of amazing power: Alderman and McCurdy like modern Larwoods – just as people here came to think during the disasters of 1984 that if only Old, Hendrick, Sidebottom had been available everything would have been all right.

Australia have not lost any world beaters, but they have lost players who would have given their selectors different options in the months ahead. And if the team does badly when India and New Zealand go to Australia later this year, their spectators will not sit transfixed, as English cricket followers did: they will desert the game and push off to the beach.

For Australia's present set of players, the danger is that they will forget how to win games. Their latest pummelling fell into three phases. On Saturday morning their tail-enders and Ritchie fell only 24 runs short of saving Gower a decision about the follow-on.

In the afternoon the rain came, then, on a soft and sun-kissed evening, Australia started to disintegrate all over again. One by one, the boys of summer 1985 made their final exits as Botham – the pain now supposedly out of his knee and into his big toe – ripped into them at a pace not that far short of West Indian quick.

Wood, who has had a wretched series except for Trent Bridge, chopped on; Wessels drove at an absurdly wide ball and was victim of Downton's best catch of the series; Wellham anticipated an outswinger from Ellison and anticipated wrong.

In between, Hilditch departed. Since his marvellous perform-ance at Headingley, he has not passed 50, partly due to being hooked on the hook. He was determined not to do it this time. The Melbourne Age correspondent compared Hilditch to a drunk attending his first alcoholics anonymous meeting, trying desper-ately not to reach for his hipflask. The strain was too much, an attempted drive dollied to gully.

Border and Ritchie, the batsmen who won the Lord's Test, are still there. Where there's life, I suppose, there's some hope for Australia; there has as yet been no sign of a marked deterioration in the pitch. But the chances are that the end will be quick and clean.

Had it not rained, Australia might have lost inside three days, and the 16,000 who have paid for today would have been furious – only bad weather is covered by the guarantee, not bad play. Now with luck, a packed house, rather than the usual Tuesday handful, should be present to see one of the historic days of English cricket.

FOURTH DAY

The Oval, Tuesday 3 September

The end came with extraordinary rapidity. Australia were 129 all out, losing their last six wickets in only 95 minutes yesterday and before even getting a chance to unpack their picnics, the crowd were filing across The Oval outfield to hear the speeches or, rather, this being 1985, the TV interviews.

England had won the final Test by an innings and 94, the first time since 1956 they have beaten Australia by an innings twice running. The Ashes are back by three Tests to one and England have won three successive home series against Australia for the first time since W.G.'s day in the 1890s.

The packed house gave the occasion a flavour it would have lost had Australia resisted into Tuesday. But the spectators were as good as gold. Only three youths attempted the old trick of dashing on as the final wicket fell. Everyone else filed stoically towards the pavilion in the great British queuing tradition; there was no way of telling from their demeanour which side had won.

David Gower then appeared on the balcony and gave a Princess Di wave, half-regal, half-shy. The interviewer, Peter West, mentioned The Oval's most famous balcony-crowd scene, 1953, when England, under Hutton, won the Ashes for the first time since the war. Gower looked blank and said he wasn't born then.

But later, in the quiet of the Surrey Library with W.G. staring down at him, Gower had enough sense of history to say it was the greatest moment of his career. He was also man of the series for his 732 runs (Gooch was man of this particular match). No one, contemplating Gower's form at the start of the summer, could have predicted that – it is the greatest comeback since Charles II.

Border's first answer to West was drowned in the applause from the throng; recognition for a very worthy opponent indeed. Gower thought that summed up the amity of the series, which it did, as did the sneak pictures in yesterday's papers. Border, late on Saturday in Mayfair, was accompanied not by the traditional Mayfair sort of companion but by Botham. The 1985 Australians have delighted everyone with their affability towards the opponents and their please-and-thank-you to everyone.

Alas, not with their cricket, though. Border yesterday would not even argue with the idea that the Australians were the weakest ever. He thought the 1981 side, which also lost 3–1, was much stronger, with Lillee and Alderman, and wondered aloud whether experienced batsmen like Hughes and Yallop might not have given the team more body. But, essentially, he thought Australia's bowling weaknesses were decisive. 'We never really got it together with the old line and length, the basics of bowling, and England scored at a fantastic rate.'

Gower thought the balance of England's attack, in the last couple of Tests, had been a great asset. This included Botham operating as a genuine quick bowler, which again is not something that could have been easily predicted on recent form.

He also noted the batsmen's new habit of making big centuries. There were eight England hundreds in the series, but no Englishman was out anywhere between 86 and 148. 'When things go right,' Gower said, enunciating a new doctrine, 'make the most of it. Get greedy.'

The last phase of the series yesterday belonged primarily to the Lion of Edgbaston, Richard Ellison, who finished with five for 46 to give him 17 in the past two Tests. But the Australians might have got out to anyone yesterday.

The management was annoyed at the start, following reports that they had refused to play in the hypothetical beer match if the Test finished early. The TCCB were offering £10,000 prize money, twice as much as England got for winning the real game, and it was Gower who rejected the idea, partly out of superstition, partly because he thought his players had done enough.

Some thought the Australians played at the end as though they were in a beer match already: Ritchie was caught behind, driving; then Phillips's square-cut, which has given England more wickets than the Hilditch hook (though it has given him plenty of runs too), brought Botham his 31st victim of the series. Then Border, who has spent the summer like Horatius on the bridge while Lars Porsena Botham scared off everyone else, edged a slanting Ellison delivery to second slip, and England were through.

The last three wickets fell in two overs. Lawson drove at a wide one. Botham took a cat-like slip catch to dismiss McDermott, and when the clouds came over and the umpires offered the last two

The crowd restrained, Botham unrestrained, as Gower lifts the replica of the Ashes.

Botham brilliantly clings on to a slip catch offered by McDermott, and the
Australians are almost beaten.

batsmen the light, they did not think it was worth the bother of
going in.

It was so dark that Bennett removed his customary sunglasses
before giving Taylor the soft return catch that settled the match
(an hour later it was raining hard). Even without Bennett's specs,
the field now was full of shades – of 1953 and 1926, of Hutton
and Percy Chapman, the only other England captains to recapture
the Ashes on this ground. Despite all the weaknesses, many of the
performances in this series are fit to rank in the pantheon: the
batting of Border, Ritchie, Gooch, Robinson, Gatting and, above
all, Gower; the bowling of McDermott, Ellison and Botham.

The last drenching of summer: from left, Lamb, Gatting, Botham, Gower and Downton.

For Gower, even greater glory beckons. For once, England have a long holiday. Their next Test, in Kingston, is on February 21. That will be the first of 15 tests in 1986, and the players will probably not have a break longer than a month until 1988.

By then, if they can take the pace, England might just be established as the world's leading cricketing nation. Gower joked yesterday about the West Indies 'quaking in their boots' but with Garner and Holding on the far side of the mountain-top and the always-fragile cohesion of the West Indians in doubt after Lloyd's retirement, there is just a chance it is not such a joke.

For now, though, England are just delighted with their achievement. And rightly so. There has been, to nick the title of Mike Brearley's account of the 1981 series, a phoenix from these Ashes too: it is David Gower.

England v. Australia

SIXTH TEST

at The Oval, Thursday, Friday, Saturday, Monday & Tuesday, 29, 30, 31 Aug. 2 & 3 Sept. 1985

Any alterations to teams will be announced over the public address system.

ENGLAND

	First Innings		Second Innings
1 G. A. Gooch (Essex)	c & b McDermott	196	
2 R. T. Robinson (Nottinghamshire)	b McDermott	3	
*3 D. I. Gower (Leicestershire)	c Bennett b McDermott	157	
4 M. W. Gatting (Middlesex)	c Border b Bennett	4	
8 J. E. Emburey (Middlesex)	c Welham b Lawson	9	
5 A. Lamb (Northamptonshire)	c McDermott b Lawson	1	
6 I. T. Botham (Somerset)	c Phillips b Lawson	12	
‡7 P. R. Downton (Middlesex)	b McDermott	16	
10 R. M. Ellison (Kent)	c Phillips b Gilbert	3	
9 P. H. Edmonds (Middlesex)	lbw b Lawson	12	
11 L. B. Taylor (Leicestershire)	not out	1	
	B13, l-b11, w , n-b26	50	B , l-b , w , n-b
	Total (118·2 overs)	464	Total

Fall of wickets—First Innings 1—20 ... 2—371 ... 3—376 ... 4—403 ... 5—405 ... 6—418 ... 7—425 ... 8—447 ... 9—452 ... 10—464
Second Innings 1— ... 2— ... 3— ... 4— ... 5— ... 6— ... 7— ... 8— ... 9— ... 10—

Bowling Analysis 1st Innings	O.	M.	R.	W.	Wd.	N.b.	2nd. Innings	O.	M.	R.	W.	Wd.	N.b.
Lawson	29·2	6	101	4		9							
McDermott	31	2	108	4		7							
Gilbert	21	2	96	1		10							
Bennett	32	8	111	1									
Border	2	0	8	0									
Wessels	3	0	16	0									

AUSTRALIA

	First Innings		Second Innings	
1 G. M. Wood (W. Australia)	lbw b Botham	22	b Botham	6
2 A. M. J. Hilditch (S. Australia)	c Gooch b Botham	17	c Gower b Taylor	9
3 K. C. Wessels (Queensland)	b Emburey	12	c Downton b Botham	7
*4 A. R. Border (Queensland)	b Edmonds	38	c Botham b Ellison	58
5 D. M. Welham (N. S. W.)	c Downton b Ellison	13	lbw b Ellison	5
6 G. M. Ritchie (Queensland)	not out	64	c Downton b Ellison	6
‡7 W. B. Phillips (S. Australia)	b Edmonds	18	c Downton b Botham	10
9 M. J. Bennett (N. S. W.)	c Robinson b Ellison	12	c & b Taylor	11
8 G. F. Lawson (N. S. W.)	c Botham b Taylor	14	c Downton b Ellison	7
10 C. J. McDermott (Queensland)	run out	25	c Botham b Ellison	2
11 D. R. Gilbert (N. S. W.)	b Botham	1	not out	0
	B , l-b3 , w2, n-b	5	B4, l-b , w , n-b4	8
	Total (84 overs)	241	Total (46·3 overs)	129

Fall of wickets—First Innings 1—35 ... 2—52 ... 3—56 ... 4—101 ... 5—109 ... 6—144 ... 7—171 ... 8—192 ... 9—235 ... 10—241
Second Innings 1—13 ... 2—16 ... 3—37 ... 4—51 ... 5—71 ... 6—96 ... 7—114 ... 8—127 ... 9—129 ... 10—129

Bowling Analysis 1st Innings	O.	M.	R.	W.	Wd.	N.b.	2nd. Innings	O.	M.	R.	W.	Wd.	N.b.
Botham	20	3	64	3	2			17	3	41	3		1
Taylor	13	1	39	1				11·3	1	34	2		3
Ellison	18	5	35	2				17	3	46	5		
Emburey	19	7	48	1				1	0	1	0		
Edmonds	14	2	52	2									

*Captain   ‡Wkt.-keeper   Scorers: T. Billson & M. P. Ringham   Umpires—H. D. Bird & K. E. Palmer   Toss won by—ENGLAND

NEW BALL: the fielding team may not claim a new ball until 85 overs have been bowled   RESULT—England won by an Innings and 94 runs

Hours of play: 11.00 a.m.—6.00 p.m. or after 90 overs have been bowled whichever is the later.   In the event of play being suspended for 1 hour or more on any of the first four days, play may continue until 7.00 p.m.   Lunch: 1.00 p.m.—1.40 p.m.   Tea: 3.40 p.m.—4.00 p.m.

Man of the Match: Graham Gooch   Man of the Series: David Gower

APPENDIX

ENGLAND

David Gower, Leicestershire, captain. Born Tunbridge Wells, Kent, 1 April 1957

*Graham Gooch, Essex. Born Leytonstone, 23 July 1953

Graeme Fowler, Lancashire. Born Accrington, 20 April 1957

Allan Lamb, Northamptonshire. Born Langebaanweg, South Africa, 20 June 1954

Ian Botham, Somerset. Born Heswall, Cheshire, 24 November 1955

Mike Gatting, Middlesex. Born Kingsbury, 6 June 1957

*Peter Willey, Leicestershire. Born Sedgefield, County Durham, 6 December 1949

Paul Downton, Middlesex. Born Farnborough, Kent, 4 April 1957

Phillipe Edmonds, Middlesex. Born Lusaka, Zambia, 8 March 1951

Paul Allott, Lancashire. Born Altrincham, Cheshire, 14 September 1956

Norman Cowans, Middlesex. Born Enfield St Mary, Jamaica, 17 April 1961

Tim Robinson, Nottinghamshire. Born Sutton-in-Ashfield, 21 November 1958

Neil Foster, Essex. Born Colchester, 6 May 1962

*John Emburey, Middlesex. Born Peckham, South London, 20 August 1952

*Arnold Sidebottom, Yorkshire. Born Barnsley, 1 April 1954

Jonathan Agnew, Leicestershire. Born Macclesfield, Cheshire, 4 April 1960

Richard Ellison, Kent. Born Ashford, 21 September 1959

*Les Taylor, Leicestershire. Born Earl Shilton, 25 October 1953

Selectors: Peter May, chairman (Surrey and England); Alec Bedser (Surrey and England); Alan Smith (Warwickshire and England); Philip Sharpe (Yorkshire and England).

* Banned from international cricket between 1982 and April 1985 for going on the unauthorised tour of South Africa in March 1982

AUSTRALIA

Allan Border, Queensland. Born Cremorne, NSW, 27 July 1955

Andrew Hilditch, South Australia. Born Adelaide, 20 May 1956

Murray Bennett, New South Wales. Born Brisbane, Queensland, 6 October 1956

David Boon, Tasmania. Born Launceston, 29 December 1960

†David Gilbert, New South Wales. Born Sydney, 19 December 1960

Robert Holland, New South Wales. Born Newcastle, NSW, 19 October 1946

Geoff Lawson, New South Wales. Born Wagga Wagga, 7 December 1957

Craig McDermott, Queensland. Born Ipswich, Queensland, 14 April 1965

Greg Matthews, New South Wales. Born Newcastle, NSW, 15 December 1965

Simon O'Donnell, Victoria. Born Denilquin, NSW, 26 January 1963

†Ray Phillips, Queensland. Born Sydney, NSW, 23 May 1954

Wayne Phillips, South Australia. Born Adelaide, 1 March 1958

Greg Ritchie, Queensland. Born Stanthorpe, 23 January 1960

†Jeff Thomson, Queensland. Born Greenacre, NSW, 16 August 1950

Dirk Wellham, New South Wales. Born Sydney, 13 March 1959

Kepler Wessels, Queensland. Born Bloemfontein, South Africa, 14 September 1957

Graeme Wood, Western Australia. Born Perth, 6 November 1956

Manager: Bob Merriman   *Assistant manager:* Geoff Dymock

† Gilbert, Ray Phillips and Thomson were late replacements called into the party when Rod McCurdy, Steve Rixon and Terry Alderman withdrew to join the rebel squad due to tour South Africa in 1985–86

AUSTRALIAN SCORES

May 5 Arundel (one-day): DREW with Lavinia, Duchess of Norfolk's XI. Australians 261 for six dec (Ritchie 72, Border 65); Lavinia, Duchess of Norfolk's XI 148 for five.

May 8, 9, 10 Taunton: BEAT Somerset by 233 runs (*see* text).

May 11, 12, 13 (no play) Worcester: DREW with Worcestershire

Australians

A. M. J. Hilditch c Curtis b Inchmore	7
G. M. Wood lbw b Inchmore	34
†R. B. Phillips c Radford b Patel	39
G. M. Ritchie c Rhodes b Inchmore	21
*A. R. Border c Illingworth b Radford	135
D. C. Boon not out	73
G. R. J. Matthews not out	23
Extras: (b 10, lb 9, w 1, nb 12)	32
Total for five	364

Fall of wickets: 28, 55, 85, 198, 302

M. J. Bennett, G. F. Lawson, C. J. McDermott and D. R. Gilbert did not bat.

Bowling: Radford 15-0-77-1; Inchmore 18-6-38-3; Weston 4-1-16-0; Patel 20-2-90-1; Newport 12-0-72-0; Illingworth 16-7-47-0; D'Oliveira 1-0-5-0.

Worcestershire

M. J. Weston c Hilditch b McDermott	11	c Phillips b Lawson	31
T. S. Curtis c and b Bennett	76	c Wood b Lawson	10
D. M. Smith c Lawson b McDermott	0		
D. N. Patel c Ritchie b Matthews	30	lbw b Lawson	4
*P. A. Neale c Boon b Matthews	108	not out	13
D. B. D'Oliveira c Ritchie b Bennett	0	(3) b Gilbert	11
P. J. Newport not out	29	(6) not out	14
†S. J. Rhodes not out	20		
Extras (b 6, lb 5, w 2, nb 16)	29	Extras (lb 1, w 4, nb 5)	10
Total for six	303	Total for four	93

Fall of wickets: 18, 19, 81, 193, 213, 273

J. D. Inchmore, N. V. Radford and R. K. Illingworth did not bat.

Bowling: Lawson 13-1-65-0; McDermott 13-3-39-2; Gilbert 19-1-90-0; Matthews 23.5-8-55-2; Bennett 19-8-43-2.

Fall of wickets: 40, 50, 58, 71.

Bowling: McDermott 2-0-22-0; Gilbert 14.2-2-49-1; Lawson 7-3-11-3; Bennett 6-2-10-0.

Umpires: D. J. Constant and K. E. Palmer.

May 14 Trent Bridge (one-day): ABANDONED v. Notts without a ball being bowled.

May 16 The Oval (one-day): LOST to Surrey by six wickets, Australians 216 for seven, 55 overs (W. Phillips 66); Surrey 217 for four, 54.1 overs (Clinton 86, Butcher 64).

May 18, 19, 20, 21   Hove: DREW with Sussex

Australians

*A. M. J. Hilditch c Gould b Le Roux	8	(2) c Waller by C. M. Wells	0
G. M. Wood lbw b Imran	8	(1) c sub b Waller	18
K. C. Wessels c C. M. Wells b Waller	56	run out	18
G. M. Ritchie run out	16	(5) not out	100
D. C. Boon c A. P. Wells b C. M. Wells	119	(4) c sub b Greig	21
†W. B. Phillips c Parker b Barclay	33	c Greig b Green	91
G. R. J. Matthews lbw b Imran	19	c sub b Waller	1
S. P. O'Donnell not out	37	not out	15
R. G. Holland c Parker b Greig	4		
D. R. Gilbert b Barclay	7		
J. R. Thomson b Imran	3		
Extras (b 1, lb 4, nb 6)	11	Extras (b 4, lb 2, nb 5)	11
Total	321	Total for six	275

Fall of wickets: 16, 16, 37, 135, 200, 245, 273, 282, 314

Bowling: Le Roux 10–2–19–1; Imran 21.2–10–55–3; C. M. Wells 20–5–73–1; Greig 12–2–43–1; Waller 33–9–61–1; Barclay 18–2–65–2.

Fall of wickets: 7, 37, 41, 90, 232, 235

Bowling: Imran 12–5–33–0; C. M. Wells 12–2–35–1; Waller 30–9–66–2; Greig 14–4–47–1; Green 21.3–4–76–1; Parker 1–0–12–0.

Sussex

G. D. Mendis c and b Holland	81	c Gilbert b Thomson	7
A. M. Green b Gilbert	27	c Phillips b Holland	29
P. W. G. Parker b Matthews	26	(4) b O'Donnell	12
A. P. Wells c Hilditch b Matthews	0	(5) c Ritchie b Holland	5
C. M. Wells b Holland	38	(6) lbw b Holland	0
Imran Khan c Holland b O'Donnell	0	(7) not out	44
*J. R. T. Barclay retired hurt	37	(8) b Matthews	19
I. A. Greig lbw b Gilbert	8	(9) b Matthews	15
†I. J. Gould b Gilbert	0	(10) b Holland	2
G. S. Le Roux c Phillips b Gilbert	20	(11) not out	0
C. E. Waller not out	2	(3) b Gilbert	8
Extras (lb 3, w 1, nb 19)	23	Extras (lb 7, nb 6)	12
Total	262	Total for nine	153

Fall of wickets: 54, 119, 121, 181, 186, 198, 213, 215, 254

Bowling: Thomson 13.3–4–50–0; Gilbert 32–6–97–4; O'Donnell 14–4–25–1; Holland 23–5–49–2; Matthews 11–3–38–2.

Fall of wickets: 11, 31, 59, 59, 59, 66, 105, 137, 146

Bowling: Thomson 7–1–31–1; Gilbert 7–2–15–1; O'Donnell 9–0–27–1; Holland 20–10–37–4; Matthews 11–2–36–2.

Umpires: D. G. L. Evans and J. H. Harris

May 22, 23, 24   Lord's: DREW with MCC (*see* text).

May 25, 26 (no play), *27* (no play) Derby: DREW v. Derbyshire

Australians

A. M. J. Hilditch c Maher b Miller	60
G. M. Wood c Roberts b Miller	16
D. M. Wellham c Maher b Moir	77
*A. R. Border c Wright b Moir	100
D. C. Boon not out	10
G. R. J. Matthews lbw b Miller	1
†W. B. Phillips not out	0
Extras (b 3, lb 4, w 1, nb 6)	14
Total for five	278

Fall of wickets: 38, 96, 244, 274, 277

M. J. Bennett, D. R. Gilbert, R. G. Holland and C. J. McDermott did not bat.

Bowling: Newman 7–2–27–0; Finney 14–1–52–0; Miller 39–5–125–3; Moir 27–7–67–2.

Derbyshire

*K. J. Barnett, A. Hill, J. E. Morris, B. Roberts, J. G. Wright, W. P. Fowler, G. Miller, R. J. Finney, †B. J. M. Maher, D. G. Moir, P. G. Newman.

Umpires: H. D. Bird and B. J. Meyer.

The match was abandoned after three of the scheduled four days and a 55-over match arranged instead.

May 28 Derby (one-day): BEAT Derbyshire by six wickets. Derbyshire 188 for nine, 55 overs (Barnett 54, Matthews 11–2–20–1); Australians 192 for four, 52.4 overs (Wessels 64, Miller 11–4–12–0).

May 30 Old Trafford (one-day) FIRST ONE-DAY INTERNATIONAL: BEAT England by three wickets (*see* text).

June 1 Edgbaston (one-day) SECOND ONE-DAY INTERNATIONAL: BEAT England by four wickets (*see* text).

June 3 Lord's (one-day) THIRD ONE-DAY INTERNATIONAL: LOST to England by eight wickets (*see* text).

June 5, 6 (no play), *7* Headingley: DREW with Yorkshire

Australians

*A. M. J. Hilditch c Blakey b Fletcher	18
G. M. Wood not out	102
D. M. Wellham c Carrick b Pickles	8
G. M. Ritchie not out	58
Extras (lb 4, w 3, nb 2)	9
Total for two	195

Fall of wickets: 33, 53

D. C. Boon, S. P. O'Donnell, †R. B. Phillips, M. J. Bennett, C. J. McDermott, R. G. Holland and D. R. Gilbert did not bat.

Bowling: Fletcher 13–2–48–1; Shaw 19–5–56–0; Pickles 14–6–40–1; Hartley 12.5–4–38–0; Carrick 3–1–9–0.

Yorkshire

G. Boycott not out	52
R. J. Blakey c Phillips b McDermott	31
K. Sharp c Hilditch b Bennett	24
J. D. Love not out	1
Extras (b 4, lb 4, nb 8)	16
Total for two	124

Fall of wickets: 70, 122

*†D. L. Bairstow, S. N. Hartley, P. Carrick, P. A. Booth, C. S. Pickles, C. Shaw and S. D. Fletcher did not bat.

Bowling: McDermott 15–2–49–1; Gilbert 12–3–36–0; Bennett 8–3–14–1; O'Donnell 5–1–17–0.

Umpires: D. O. Oslear and B. Leadbeater.

June 8, 9, 10, 11 Leicester: DREW with Leicestershire

Australians

K. C. Wessels lbw b Agnew	2
A. M. J. Hilditch c Butcher b Willey	56
D. C. Boon b Agnew	39
†W. B. Phillips c Cook b Willey	128
G. M. Ritchie b Parsons	115
*A. R. Border b Taylor	25
G. R. J. Matthews b Cook	26
C. J. McDermott not out	53
R. G. Holland b Agnew	5
J. R. Thomson b Parsons	2
G. F. Lawson absent ill	
Extras (b 4, lb 4, nb 7)	15
Total	466

Fall of wickets: 6, 66, 111, 288, 337, 388, 437, 453, 466.

Bowling: Agnew 26–2–144–3; Taylor 16–3–72–1; Parsons 28–6–88–2; Cook 29–9–87–1; Willey 18–3–67–2.

Leicestershire

I. P. Butcher b McDermott	35	not out	19
J. C. Balderstone c Ritchie b Thomson	134	not out	7
*D. I. Gower c Boon b McDermott	135		
P. Willey c Boon b McDermott	2		
J. J. Whitaker c Phillips b Thomson	18		
N. E. Briers lbw b Holland	13		
†M. A. Garnham not out	27		
G. J. Parsons b Thomson	7		
N. G. B. Cook c Phillips b Thomson	1		
J. P. Agnew c Boon b Thomson	19		
L. B. Taylor c and b Matthews	11		
Extras (b 2, lb 12, w 2, nb 36)	52	Extras (lb 1, w 1)	2
Total	454	Total for nought	28

Fall of wickets: 62, 315, 328, 353, 372, 382, 392, 394, 427.

Bowling: Lawson 15–0–71–0; Thomson 24–6–103–5; McDermott 28–3–87–3; Holland 32–4–112–1; Matthews 10.5–3–67–1.

Bowling: Wessels 5–0–9–0; Boon 3–0–12–0; Holland 2–0–5–0; Ritchie 0.3–0–1–0.

Umpires: B. Dudleston and R. Palmer.

June 13, 14, 15, 17, 18   Headingley FIRST TEST: LOST to England by five wickets (*see* text).

June 20   Cambridge (one-day): BEAT Combined Universities by 79 runs. Australians 265 for eight, 55 overs (Boon 108); Universities 186 for six, 55 overs (Roebuck 75*, Bennett 4–26).

June 22 (no play), *23, 24, 25*   Southampton: DREW with Hampshire

Australians

G. M. Wood b Connor	5	(2) c Parks b Connor	0
K. C. Wessels b James	6	(1) c Parks b Connor	6
G. M. Ritchie lbw b James	3	(4) c Connor b Maru	62
D. C. Boon lbw b James	0	(3) c Parks b Connor	0
*A. R. Border c Parks b James	8	c Connor b Maru	21
M. J. Bennett c Nicholas b Maru	13	(7) not out	16
G. F. Lawson c Cowley b James	6	(8) lbw b Maru	0
C. J. McDermott b Connor	5	(9) not out	17
R. G. Holland c R. A. Smith b James	0		
D. R. Gilbert not out	6		
†W. B. Phillips b Maru	15	(6) c James b Cowley	22
Extras (lb 1, w 2, nb 6)	9	Extras (b 2, lb 3, nb 5)	10
Total	76	Total for seven	154

Fall of wickets: 7, 12, 18, 18, 28, 37, 42, 43, 60.
Bowling: Connor 16–2–46–2; James 11–2–22–6; Maru 4.5–3–7–2.

Fall of wickets: 1, 1, 19, 64, 104, 126, 126.
Bowling: Connor 4–0–27–3; James 5–1–26–0; Cowley 13–4–49–1; Maru 13–3–41–3; C. L. Smith 1–0–2–0; R. A. Smith 1–0–4–0.

Hampshire

V. P. Terry lbw b Holland	60		
C. L. Smith c Phillips b McDermott	29	not out	41
*M. C. J. Nicholas c Wood b Bennett	17	(1) c Wood b Ritchie	5
R. A. Smith b Holland	5	(3) not out	17
J. J. E. Hardy lbw b Holland	27		
K. D. James c Phillips b Lawson	8		
†R. J. Parks b Holland	33		
N. G. Cowley lbw b Holland	11		
R. J. Maru c Boon b McDermott	4		
C. A. Connor not out	4		
S. J. W. Andrew retired hurt	1		
Extras (b 6, lb 2, w 2, nb 12)	22	Extras (b 1)	1
Total	221	Total for one	64

Fall of wickets: 62, 98, 120, 121, 150, 174, 200, 215, 215.
Bowling: Lawson 9–5–10–1; Gilbert 14–5–35–0; McDermott 12.2–1–39–2; Bennett 33–11–78–1; Holland 22–8–51–5.

Fall of wicket: 22.
Bowling: Lawson 2–2–0–0; Wessels 8–2–26–0; Ritchie 5–0–22–1; Boon 2–0–15–0.
Umpires: C. Cook and P. B. Wright.

June 27, 28, 29, July 1, 2   Lord's   SECOND TEST: BEAT England by four wickets (*see* text).

July 6, 7, 8, 9 Chelmsford: DREW with Essex

Australians

G. M. Wood c Lilley b Gooch	33	(2) c East b Pringle	8
*A. M. J. Hilditch c Pringle b Foster	80	(1) c Pringle b Foster	35
K. C. Wessels b Gooch	23	c East b Pringle	0
D. M. Wellham c Acfield b Phillip	10	b Foster	63
D. C. Boon c Gooch b Foster	21	b Gooch	138
S. P. O'Donnell c and b Gooch	39	b Pringle	31
G. R. J. Matthews b Acfield	5	c East b Gooch	6
†R. B. Phillips c and b Phillip	28	b Gooch	9
M. J. Bennett lbw b Phillip	23	c East b Gooch	0
D. R. Gilbert not out	6	b Pringle	7
J. R. Thomson b Phillip	1	not out	21
Extras (b 2, lb 6, nb 2)	10	Extras (b 5, lb 4, w 1, nb 5)	15
Total	279	Total	333

Fall of wickets: 105, 125, 142, 155, 182, 217, 217, 261, 277.

Fall of wickets: 41, 45, 49, 211, 273, 291, 296, 296, 303.

Bowling: Foster 27–6–96–2; Phillip 18.5–4–55–4; Acfield 18–5–36–1; Pringle 26–7–43–0; Gooch 21–7–41–3.

Bowling: Foster 20–3–92–2; Phillip 7–0–39–0; Pringle 27–5–69–4; Gooch 19.3–3–61–4; Acfield 22–6–58–0; Lilley 1–0–5–0.

Essex

*G. A. Gooch c Hilditch b Matthews	68	c Boon b Gilbert	27
C. Gladwin c O'Donnell b Gilbert	5	lbw b Matthews	27
P. J. Prichard c Phillips b Gilbert	7	c Phillips b Gilbert	4
A. W. Lilley lbw b Gilbert	15	(7) c Wessels b Matthews	11
D. R. Pringle c Phillips b Thomson	29	c Phillips b Gilbert	4
B. R. Hardie not out	113	b Thomson	17
K. S. McEwan c and b Bennett	18	(4) lbw b Gilbert	0
N. Phillip c Matthews b Thomson	50	c Wood b Thomson	22
†D. E. East c Wessels b Thomson	23	not out	30
N. A. Foster c Phillips b Matthews	14	not out	15
D. L. Acfield c and b Matthews	14		
Extras (b 12, lb 8, w 5, nb 28)	53	Extras (lb 10, nb 2)	12
Total	409	Total for eight	169

Fall of wickets: 21, 53, 91, 131, 146, 192, 299, 345, 389.

Fall of wickets: 40, 56, 56, 62, 66, 85, 123, 124.

Bowling: Thomson 24–2–93–3; Gilbert 23–2–90–3; O'Donnell 15–1–58–0; Bennett 26–4–72–1; Matthews 15.4–1–76–3.

Bowling: Thomson 16–2–46–2; Gilbert 21–9–41–4; O'Donnell 4–0–22–0; Matthews 17–7–42–2; Bennett 4–2–8–0.

Umpires: J. H. Hampshire and M. J. Kitchen.

July 11, 12, 13, 15, 16 Trent Bridge THIRD TEST: DREW with England (*see* text).

July 18 Jesmond one-day: BEAT Minor Counties by 125 runs. Australians 331 for two, 55 overs (Wellham 107*, Boon 84*, Wood 83); Minor Counties 206 for seven, 55 overs (Roope 76).

July 20, 21, 22 (no play)   Neath: DREW with Glamorgan

Australians

*A. M. J. Hilditch lbw b Thomas	15
G. M. Wood not out	38
D. M. Wellham not out	43
Extras (b 5, nb 2, w 2)	9
Total for one	105

Fall of wicket: 42.

D. C. Boon, G. M. Ritchie, G. R. J. Matthews, M. J. Bennett, †R. B. Phillips, C. J. McDermott, J. R. Thomson and D. R. Gilbert did not bat.

Bowling: Thomas 10-4-49-1; Barwick 9.4-1-31-0; Younis 7-3-20-0.

Glamorgan

J. A. Hopkins c and b Bennett	30
A. L. Jones b Bennett	24
G. C. Holmes c and b Bennett	5
Javed Miandad not out	200
Younis Ahmed not out	118
Extras (b 3, lb 9, w 5, nb 15)	32
Total for three	409

Fall of wickets: 48, 62, 103

H. Morris, *R. C. Ontong, †T. Davies, M. R. Price, J. G. Thomas and S. R. Barwick did not bat.

Bowling: McDermott 14-4-55-0; Thomson 12-1-53-0; Bennett 25.4-5-101-3; Gilbert 18-0-99-0; Matthews 21-3-83-0; Boon 1-0-6-0.

Umpires: B. Dudleston and N. T. Plews.

July 24, 25, 26   Bristol: BEAT Gloucestershire by 170 runs

Australians

K. C. Wessels b Lawrence	0	not out	61
W. B. Phillips c Bainbridge b Curran	22	b Walsh	48
D. M. Wellham c Russell b Lawrence	10	b Graveney	105
*A. R. Border c Russell b Walsh	5	c Stovold b Graveney	130
S. P. O'Donnell b Walsh	3	not out	31
G. R. J. Matthews not out	41		
†R. B. Phillips c Russell b Curran	23		
G. F. Lawson b Lawrence	0		
R. G. Holland b Curran	0		
J. R. Thomson b Curran	10		
D. R. Gilbert b Curran	12		
Extras (b 4, lb 5, nb 11)	20	Extras (b 15, lb 9, w 1, nb 10)	35
Total	146	Total for three	410

Fall of wickets: 0, 28, 42, 44, 48, 110, 111, 112, 123.

Bowling: Lawrence 12-1-52-3; Walsh 11-2-33-2; Curran 12-4-35-5; Bainbridge 3-0-17-0.

Fall of wickets: 98, 334, 339.

Bowling: Lawrence 16-0-89-0; Walsh 9-0-37-1; Curran 12-0-43-0; Lloyds 13-0-83-0; Bainbridge 8-0-34-0; Graveney 20-1-100-2.

Gloucestershire

A. W. Stovold lbw b Lawson	16	c Holland b Thomson	8
P. W. Romaines c R. B. Phillips b Thomson	6	c R. B. Phillips b Thomson	0
A. J. Wright lbw b Lawson	4	b Thomson	9
C. W. J. Athey lbw b Lawson	0	b Holland	83
P. Bainbridge c Border b Gilbert	23	b O'Donnell	25
K. M. Curran c Wessels b Thomson	25	lbw b Gilbert	58
J. W. Lloyds c sub b Holland	71	c Wessels b Holland	0
*D. A. Graveney lbw b O'Donnell	23	not out	4
D. V. Lawrence b O'Donnell	1	b Gilbert	0
C. A. Walsh not out	2	b Holland	4
†R. C. Russell absent injured		absent injured	
Extras (lb 2, nb 8)	10	Extras (b 5, lb 6, w 2, nb 1)	14
Total	181	Total	205

Fall of wickets: 22, 29, 29, 32, 73, 79, 167, 177, 181.

Fall of wickets: 1, 12, 23, 70, 178, 178, 200, 200, 205.

Bowling: Lawson 10–0–42–3; Thomson 10–1–36–2; Gilbert 16–1–63–1; Holland 8–2–26–1; O'Donnell 8–1–12–2.

Bowling: Thomson 9–2–38–3; Gilbert 13–1–55–2; O'Donnell 10–5–13–1; Matthews 10–2–32–0; Holland 13.2–2–56–3.

Umpires: B. J. Meyer and D. R. Shepherd.

July 27, 28, 29, 30 (no play)   Northampton: DREW with Northamptonshire

Australians

*A. M. J. Hilditch lbw b Griffiths	0
G. M. Wood retired hurt	20
K. C. Wessels c Lamb b Wheeler	1
D. C. Boon not out	206
G. M. Ritchie run out	49
†W. B. Phillips b Williams	55
S. P. O'Donnell b Capel	8
G. R. J. Matthews not out	51
Extras (b 2, lb 10, w 2)	14
Total for five	404

Fall of wickets: 4, 13, 109, 215, 254.

M. J. Bennett, C. J. McDermott and R. G. Holland did not bat.

Bowling: Griffiths 25–5–72–1; Wheeler 20–0–87–1; Capel 22–0–107–1; Larkins 6–0–26–0; Williams 21–5–66–1; Harper 11–3–27–0; Lamb 2–0–7–0.

Northamptonshire

*G. Cook lbw b McDermott	24
W. Larkins c sub b O'Donnell	44
R. J. Boyd-Moss c Phillips b McDermott	18
R. J. Bailey not out	107
R. G. Williams not out	35
Extras (b 12, lb 11, nb 7)	30
Total for three	258

Fall of wickets: 53, 82, 149

A. J. Lamb, D. J. Capel, †D. Ripley, R. A. Harper, M. B. H. Wheeler and B. J. Griffiths did not bat.

Bowling: McDermott 19–3–70–2; O'Donnell 16–1–81–1; Bennett 14–3–43–0; Holland 7–3–12–0; Matthews 13.2–3–29–0.

Umpires: J. W. Holder and A. A. Jones.

August 1, 2, 3, 5, 6   Old Trafford FOURTH TEST: DREW with England (*see* text).

August 8   Downpatrick (one-day): DREW with Ireland. Australia 151 for four (Border 91).

August 10, 11, 12, 13   Lord's: DREW with Middlesex

Australians

G. M. Wood c Edmonds b Gatting	42
K. C. Wessels c Radley b Gatting	56
D. C. Boon lbw b Gatting	4
D. M. Wellham not out	125
G. M. Ritchie b Hughes	27
†W. B. Phillips c and b Edmonds	73
M. J. Bennett c Emburey b Edmonds	7
*G. F. Lawson not out	29
Extras (b 10, lb 5, w 5, nb 13)	33
	—
Total for six	396

Fall of wickets: 107, 111, 116, 168, 319, 329.

C. J. McDermott, J. R. Thomson and R. G. Holland did not bat.

Bowling: Williams 17-0-85-0; Cowans 17-3-72-0; Hughes 20-1-61-1; Gatting 13-1-55-3; Emburey 22-5-55-0; Edmonds 19-4-46-2; Brown 1-1-0-0; Butcher 1-0-7-0.

Middlesex

W. N. Slack not out	201
K. R. Brown st Phillips b Bennett	102
*M. W. Gatting b McDermott	7
R. O. Butcher lbw b Holland	0
C. T. Radley c Wood b Bennett	34
†P. R. Downton not out	24
Extras (b 4, lb 6, w 2, nb 17)	29
	—
Total for four	397

Fall of wickets: 213, 251, 252, 344.

J. E. Emburey, P. H. Edmonds, N. F. Williams, S. P. Hughes and N. G. Cowans did not bat.

Bowling: McDermott 25-3-108-1; Lawson 20-8-39-0; Thomson 18-4-54-0; Holland 30-3-87-1; Bennett 38-5-95-2; Wessels 3-1-4-0.

Umpires: D. O. Oslear and R. A. White.

August 15, 16, 17, 19, 20   Edgbaston FIFTH TEST: LOST to England by an innings and 118 runs (*see* text).

August 24, 25, 26, 27   Canterbury: BEAT Kent by seven wickets.

Australians

G. M. Wood c Marsh b Baptiste	8	c Marsh b Baptiste	18
A. M. J. Hilditch c Marsh b Ellison	16	c Potter b Cowdrey	9
K. C. Wessels c Marsh b Ellison	51		
D. M. Wellham b Ellison	1	(3) c Hinks b Baptiste	38
G. M. Ritchie c Hinks b Potter	155		
*A. R. Border c Marsh b Baptiste	103		
†R. B. Phillips c Marsh b Baptiste	8	(4) not out	23
M. J. Bennett c Hinks b Underwood	8	(5) not out	9
C. J. McDermott b Baptiste	5		
D. R. Gilbert c C. Cowdrey b Underwood	0		
J. R. Thomson not out	0		
Extras (b 1, lb 3, w 1, nb 4)	9	Extras (lb 1, nb 1)	2
Total	364	Total for three	99

Fall of wickets: 24, 24, 79, 138, 320, 343, 350, 364, 364.

Fall of wickets: 9, 61, 66.

Bowling: Baptiste 27–7–89–4; Ellison 15–2–43–3; C. Cowdrey 4–1–19–0; Hinks 12–1–48–0; Underwood 31–6–71–2; Potter 19–3–90–1.

Bowling: Baptiste 10–0–36–2; C. Cowdrey 6–1–16–1; Potter 6–0–37–0; Aslett 2.1–0–9–0.

Kent

N. R. Taylor lbw b Gilbert	5	c Phillips b Gilbert	3
S. G. Hinks c Phillips b Gilbert	15	c Wessels b McDermott	0
D. G. Aslett run out	24	c Phillips b Bennett	13
L. Potter b Gilbert	58	b Bennett	28
E. A. E. Baptiste c Thomson b Bennett	45	(6) c Wood b McDermott	11
G. R. Cowdrey c Gilbert b Thomson	51	(5) b Bennett	4
R. M. Ellison run out	29	c Phillips b McDermott	27
*C. S. Cowdrey c Bennett b McDermott	35	(9) lbw b Bennett	9
†S. Marsh not out	31	(8) b McDermott	0
B. W. Luckhurst c Border b McDermott	1	not out	9
D. L. Underwood b McDermott	3	b McDermott	0
Extras (b 4, lb 6, w 2, nb 24)	36	Extras (b 4, lb 8, w 1, nb 9)	22
Total	333	Total	126

Fall of wickets: 9, 34, 57, 137, 194, 232, 271, 301, 326.

Fall of wickets: 3, 3, 42, 56, 68, 79, 81, 90, 124.

Bowling: McDermott 24–5–104–3; Gilbert 26–5–62–3; Wessels 10–4–22–0; Bennett 30–6–99–1; Hilditch 4–2–10–0; Border 2–1–1–0; Thomson 7–1–25–1.

Bowling: McDermott 11.2–3–18–5; Gilbert 17–2–57–1; Bennett 16–4–39–4.

Umpires: J. A. Jameson and B. Leadbeater.

August 29, 30, 31, September 2   The Oval SIXTH TEST: LOST to England by an innings and 94 runs (*see* text).

TEST AVERAGES

England

Batting

	M	I	NO	R	HS	Avge
M. W. Gatting	6	9	3	527	160	87.83
D. I. Gower	6	9	0	732	215	81.33
R. T. Robinson	6	9	1	490	175	61.25
G. A. Gooch	6	9	0	487	196	54.11
A. J. Lamb	6	8	1	256	67	36.57
J. E. Emburey	6	6	2	130	33	32.50
I. T. Botham	6	8	0	250	85	31.25
P. R. Downton	6	7	1	114	54	19.00
P. H. Edmonds	5	5	0	47	21	9.40
P. J. W. Allott	4	5	1	27	12	6.75

Also batted: J. P. Agnew 2*; N. G. Cowans 22*; R. M. Ellison 3; N. A. Foster 3, 0; A. Sidebottom 2; L. B. Taylor 1*; P. Willey 36, 3*.

Hundreds: Gower 3, Gatting, Robinson 2, Gooch 1.

Bowling

	O	M	R	W	Avge
Ellison	75.5	20	185	17	10.88
Botham	251.4	36	855	31	27.58
Emburey	248.4	75	544	19	28.63
Edmonds	225.5	59	549	15	36.60
Taylor	63.3	11	178	4	44.50
Allott	113	22	297	5	59.40

Also bowled: Agnew 23-2-99-0; Cowans 33-6-28-2; Foster 23-1-83-1; Gatting 5-0-16-0; Gooch 1.2-10-102-2; Lamb 1-0-10-0; Sidebottom 18.4-3-5-1.

Fielding: 20 - Downton (19 ct, 1 st); 8 - Botham, Edmonds; 7 - Lamb; 6 - Gower; 5 - Robinson; 4 - Gooch; 3 - Emburey; 1 - Ellison, Taylor.

Australia

Batting

	M	I	NO	R	HS	Avge
A. R. Border	6	11	2	597	196	66.33
G. M. Ritchie	6	11	1	422	146	42.20
A. M. J. Hilditch	6	11	0	424	119	38.54
W. B. Phillips	6	11	1	350	91	35.00
K. C. Wessels	6	11	0	368	83	33.45
G. M. Wood	5	9	0	260	172	28.88
S. P. O'Donnell	5	8	1	184	48	26.28
D. C. Boon	4	7	0	124	61	17.71
G. F. Lawson	6	9	1	119	53	14.87
C. J. McDermott	6	9	1	103	35	12.87
R. G. Holland	4	5	1	15	10	3.75
J. R. Thomson	2	4	4	38	28*	—

Also batted: M. J. Bennett 12, 11; D. R. Gilbert 1, 0*; G. R. J. Matthews 4, 17; D. M. Wellham 13, 5.

Hundreds: Border 2, Ritchie, Hilditch, Wood 1.

Bowling

	O	M	R	W	Avge
McDermott	234.2	21	901	30	30.03
Lawson	246	38	830	22	37.72
Holland	172	41	465	6	77.50
O'Donnell	145.4	31	487	6	81.16
Thomson	56	4	275	3	91.66

Also bowled: Bennett 32-8-111-1; Border 11-1-37-0; Gilbert 21-2-96-1; Matthews 9-2-21-0; Ritchie 1-0-19-0; Wessels 6-2-18-0.

Fielding: 11 - Border, Phillips; 4 - Boon; 3 - Hilditch, O'Donnell, Ritchie, Wessels; 2 - McDermott; 1 - Bennett, Holland, Thomson, Wellham, Wood.

AUSTRALIAN TOUR AVERAGES

Batting

	M	I	NO	R	HS	Avge
A. R. Border	14	21	2	1355	196	71.31
D. M. Wellham	10	16	4	669	125*	55.75
D. C. Boon	15	20	5	832	206*	55.46
G. M. Ritchie	16	23	3	1097	155	54.85
W. B. Phillips	14	22	3	899	128	47.31
S. P. O'Donnell	11	16	5	448	100*	40.72
K. C. Wessels	16	26	1	905	156	36.20
G. M. Wood	16	25	3	691	172	31.40
A. M. J. Hilditch	17	27	0	829	119	30.70
R. B. Phillips	7	7	2	130	39	26.00
G. R. J. Matthews	10	12	3	216	51*	24.00
C. J. McDermott	16	14	3	183	53*	16.63
J. R. Thomson	11	11	6	82	28*	16.40
M. J. Bennett	11	10	3	111	23	15.85
G. F. Lawson	13	13	2	154	53	14.00
D. R. Gilbert	10	8	3	39	12	7.80
R. G. Holland	13	10	1	59	35	6.55

Hundreds: Border 8; Ritchie 4; Boon 3; Wellham, Wood 2; Hilditch, O'Donnell, W. Phillips, Wessels 1.

Bowling

	O	M	R	W	Avge
McDermott	421.5	49	1609	51	31.5
Thomson	241.3	33	988	29	34.0
Holland	376	94	1017	29	35.0
Lawson	347	60	1165	31	37.5
Gilbert	253.2	41	885	21	42.1
Matthews	153.4	34	521	12	43.4
Bennett	266.4	62	766	16	47.8
O'Donnell	242.4	47	819	12	68.2

Also bowled: Boon 6–0–33–0; Border 13–2–38–0; Hilditch 7–2–29–0; Ritchie 6.3–0–33–1; Wessels 32–9–79–0.

Fielding

W. Phillips 21 (20 ct, 1 st); Border, R. Phillips 13; Boon 12; Wessels 9; Hilditch, Ritchie, Wood 7; Bennett 6; Holland, O'Donnell 5; Matthews 3; Gilbert, McDermott, Thomson 2; Lawson, Wellham 1. Substitutes took eight catches and two stumpings.

RESULTS
Played 20, Won 4, Lost 3, Drew 13.